THIS BOOK IS WORTH €25,000

EASY WAYS TO SAVE THOUSANDS OF EURO RIGHT NOW

Karl Deeter & Charlie Weston

GILL BOOKS

Gill Books

Hume Avenue

Park West

Dublin 12

www.gillbooks.ie

Gill Books is an imprint of M.H. Gill and Co.

© Karl Deeter & Charlie Weston 2017

978 07171 7563 5

Designed by www.grahamthew.com

Edited by Jane Rogers

Printed by Clays Ltd, Bungay, Suffolk

This book is typeset in Brocha Light 9.5pt on 13.5pt.

The paper used in this book comes from the wood pulp of managed forests. For every tree felled, at least one tree is planted, thereby renewing natural resources.

A CIP catalogue record for this book is available from the British Library.

5 4 3 2 1

About the Authors

Charlie Weston is a nationally recognised journalist who covers personal finance with the *Irish Independent*, the country's largest-selling daily newspaper. He is also a columnist with the *Sunday Independent*, Ireland's most read Sunday paper. Charlie is recognised as one of the country's foremost personal finance journalists. He features weekly on *The Last Word* on TodayFM, where, with host Matt Cooper, he discusses the personal finance affairs of the day. He is also a regular contributor to RTÉ radio, Newstalk and regional radio stations, as well as RTÉ television and TV3.

A scourge of the banks, he campaigns on consumer issues, with a focus on variable mortgage rates, credit unions, overcharging and high motor insurance premiums. Charlie was honoured with an Outstanding Achievement Award at the annual Business Journalists' Association of Ireland and Smurfit Business School journalism awards in 2016. He is married to Emer and they have two teenage daughters, Gillian and Helen.

Karl Deeter is also a nationally recognised commentator and journalist. His day job is in the financial services industry; he is the compliance manager of Irish Mortgage Brokers, a company he co-founded in 2004.

His background is in financial advice: he is a QFA (qualified financial adviser) and holds several professional certificates in compliance, consumer credit, insolvency, and mortgage and pension trusteeship, as well as a diploma in business and accounting with the Association of Chartered Certified Accountants (ACCA). He received his college education at Dublin Institute of Technology.

Karl has written for many major newspapers and was a regular columnist with the *News of the World*, later writing a regular column called 'Mr Money' in the *Sun on Sunday* since the paper started. He is also a columnist with the *Sunday Business Post*, the nation's pre-eminent economics and financial newspaper.

He co-wrote, with Jill Kerby, a book called *Talking Money*, which was based on a long-running radio segment on RTÉ 1, and has contributed to books on finance: *What if Ireland Defaults?* (2010); and *The Irish Property Buyers' Handbook* (2011–2015). You can hear Karl giving his trademark straight-talking contributions on every major national and local radio station and on the national television stations. His focus is on property, finance, financial regulation and financial planning.

He is married to Louise and has three children. Outside work he likes to play music; his love of Americana and bluegrass is why some of his friends refer to him as a 'hillbilly' (most of his life he has actually lived in cities and is a native of Los Angeles).

Acknowledgements

Charlie Weston

My thanks go to my most understanding and accommodating wife Emer for putting up with me during the writing of this book. The woman is a rock in my life. Our daughters Gillian and Helen also deserve gratitude.

For inspiration it is only fair to mention some excellent personal finance journalists across a range of publications whose work has provided ideas and inspiration. These include ace reporters Louise McBride, Sinead Ryan, Fiona Reddan, Niall Brady and Emma Kennedy. Many a topic in this book borrows from their work.

Irish Independent editor Fionnán Sheahan, IN&M editor-in-chief Stephen Rae, IN&M group business editor Dearbhail McDonald and *Irish Independent* business editor Donal O'Donovan are colleagues who inspire and encourage my coverage of personal finance.

Down through the years, Matt Cooper has been a great supporter, allowing me to do a weekly slot on *The Last Word* on TodayFM every Wednesday. He has correctly recognised the importance of covering stories for his listeners about the euro in their pockets.

Finally, Gill Books executives Conor Nagle and Sheila Armstrong have been understanding and patient in their dealings with two annoying newbies to the publishing game.

Karl Deeter

I owe a lot of thanks to so many people because this book was the culmination of years of work and learning.

The first person I should thank is my co-author Charlie. Without him, this project wouldn't have happened, and he also vouched for me in my first jobs in journalism. After that, it's the good (and patient) people in Gill who had enough faith in the idea to see it through.

Writing time came out of my personal time, and that means I have to thank my wife Louise who is already such a bedrock in my life. To say just how great she is in every way would take up more space than the rest of this book. Thanks to my kids, who mean everything to me, but who saw a little less of me than usual for a while during some parts of the project.

I also owe so much to my parents. My mother will be so pleased to see this book come out, and I got so many gifts in life from her. I sure wish my dad was alive to see it too, as he would have gotten a kick out of it.

My business partners Seamus Carrick and Stephen Hughes have been the glue that kept Irish Mortgage Brokers going for the last 13 years, and without them I'd probably never have attempted this.

Jill Kerby was the first to drag me through the book-writing process, and she has always been like a good luck charm to me.

Pat Farrell, Paddy Stronge, Martina Fitzgerald, Audrey Carville, Brendan Burgess, Seamus Coffey, Eddie Hobbs and Felix O'Regan have always been givers of sage advice. Simon Farrell, Martin Kavanagh and Gus Friedlander taught me loads about music, life and nothing about finance and I owe them a thank you for keeping a human edge to financial analysis.

I can't be genuinely grateful without mentioning the *News of the World*, which curated my first national column (thanks Badger and Declan Ferry). That was key to my current ongoing work with *The Irish Sun*, where McNiffe, Clarkie and now McDaid have all been good to me. I have to tip my hat to Neil Cotter, Dragon, Barry and Doyler, the crew on the picture desk and the many subs who wade through my copy.

Of course, there are people in almost every paper that I need to thank: Cormac Bourke and everybody else in the Independent; Conor Pope and everybody in *The Irish Times*; Eamon Quinn and everybody in the *Examiner*; and Helen Rogers and the folks over in the *Daily Mail*. Ian Kehoe gave me a column in the *Sunday Business Post*, and I have always been grateful for that. It's on par with how grateful I am to have Tina Marie O'Neill as my editor – she's a real gem.

Radio has been a huge part of my life, and on that basis I should also thank Newstalk for getting behind the type of financial message I became known for. Conor Brophy and Anton Savage both helped me distil it better while they were part of the group.

Then there is RTÉ, where I owe a thank you to Mary Wilson, Tom Donnelly and the team in *Drivetime* who helped me learn to speak about money in an easier to understand way, which has been an invaluable discipline.

Today FM with Matt Cooper in particular have also been so good through the years, as has Pat Kenny in both RTÉ and Newstalk. Last but not least is Scott Williams and Venetia Quick in Q102.

I always thought 'there are too many people to name' was a throwaway remark until I tried to write down the people I'd like to thank myself. It has been a reminder that I have been very lucky so far in life to know so many decent folks. I hope those I didn't get to mention all know how important they are to me.

Contents

HOW
TO USE
THIS BOOK

Saying this book is worth €25,000 may seem like a big claim. But as you will see, if you were to get the maximum savings and income from each chapter, then the book is actually worth far more – in excess of €50,000. However, we think that a fairly average person should be able to be better off by about €25,000 in total.

These gains come from a combination of one-off savings, additional income and ongoing investments. Some will be recurring, others won't be, but for the sake of giving a total sum, we are happy to say that this book is worth €25,000.

We have to stress that not every choice, option or suggestion will be available or suitable for every reader, so while we are confident that €25,000 is a fair figure, your personal figures might be far higher or lower.

For that reason we are confident that the name reflects the value of this book. Of course, you'll pay only a fraction of that sum in order to learn the tips and tricks that we have garnered over many years, in Charlie's case as a journalist covering personal finance and in Karl's case as a financial adviser.

When we were coming up with a name for a book that would both save and make you money, there were many different ideas thrown around – but the simple fact is that money talks.

So much of what we hear about personal finance is confusing, time-consuming, or sounds like a lot of hassle. What we aim to do with this book is to make it easy for you to be better off financially with just a small commitment of time on a regular basis.

If you were told to give away €20 to a random stranger every day of the year you might get upset, yet many of us do exactly that by paying over the odds, getting ripped off and doing nothing about it, and by not maximising the money we keep.

If you save €5,000 by making better choices it's like getting a raise of at least €5,000 at whatever job you do, and we have never found a person who said they wouldn't take a raise of that amount for no extra work. That's the beauty of this book; you don't really have to change much of anything you do – it's more about how you do it.

The structure is simple. Each chapter covers a single topic. We start by giving you the topic, then the expected savings you can hope for over the course of a year, and the time it will take to follow the tip. Finally, the difficulty or 'hassle factor' is given a star rating of one to five, one star being the easiest and fastest, five stars requiring the most commitment. As with many tips of the trade, there are pitfalls and things that can catch you out. Therefore, we also list some of the things you need to watch out for, the aim being to save you from having to learn the hard way (which Karl says is how he learned almost everything he knows).

If you have just ten minutes to spare, find something that has a ten-minute time frame and you can just do that in the time you have. Alternatively, if you have a little more time and would rather save €1,000, flick through the chapters, find something that can save you that amount and do that instead.

The whole point of this is to make personal finance something that works in your favour, but rather than telling you all about it in boring detail (and frankly few people care about every aspect of the subject), we just explain what you need to do in order to get the benefit of the digging about and understanding we have gained through our respective careers. Listed below are just a few of the topics discussed in this book.

ENERGY. *From taking advantage of 'new customer' discounts to simply switching to a cheaper supplier, there are savings to be made if you know where to look.*

MOTOR INSURANCE. *There are a dozen motor insurers active in the market, with credit unions involved in reselling motor cover at good rates for members. Shopping around for car cover will save you lots of money. We outline other ways to save money, such as taking advantage of telematics, taking out two-year cover, and the advantage of men getting insured with an insurer that focuses on women drivers.*

FAMILY INCOME SUPPLEMENT. *Family Income Supplement (FIS) is a weekly tax-free payment available to married or unmarried employees with children. We show you how to check if you are eligible.*

HOME INSURANCE. *Seeking out better value home cover will save the average household €156 a year, according to the Competition and Consumer Protection Commission. We give you some steps you can take to reduce the cost of cover.*

CURRENT ACCOUNTS. *Day-to-day banking has become expensive. Some people are now paying their bank €120 a year for a current account. There are ways of avoiding this expense.*

HEALTH INSURANCE. *Premium rates are rising all time, but the good news is that with hundreds of different plans in the market there are ways to save a packet on private medical cover.*

MOBILE PHONES. *There are over 500 plan options available for Irish consumers – a bewildering number. But the potential for savings is now greater than ever, and reductions in monthly bills of €25 per month are common. This means savings of €300 a year.*

MORTGAGE SWITCHING. *A householder with equity in their home can save €140,000 over the term of their loan by opting for a mortgage provider with a low rate. We tell you the steps you need to take.*

HOW TO GET A TAX REFUND. *Tax refunds average €900 for those who have never made a claim to Revenue. We show you how this could be the easiest cash you will ever make.*

CAR FINANCE. *If you are in the market for a new car, you have a few choices in terms of how to pay for it, but it pays to be aware of just what type of finance you are signing up to.*

BROADBAND. *How to get the best deal while ensuring your internet is up to speed.*

TV DEALS. *Customers who want TV, a landline and broadband in their home will find the best value by bundling these services and getting them all from the one provider.*

CREDIT CARDS. *Credit cards are weapons of money destruction. We show you ways to control their use and avoid running up big debts.*

OPTIMISE YOUR SAVINGS. *High taxes and low interest rates mean it is hard to make money from deposits, but there are ways to make some money from your savings.*

PUMP UP YOUR PENSION. *Saving for retirement is the best tax break you can get, bar none. We show you how to maximise your after-work fund.*

LIFE ASSURANCE. *There is massive competition in the life assurance market. If you have never checked out whether you can get a better deal on life cover, or mortgage protection, the likelihood is you are losing out.*

BIN CHARGES. *It's almost impossible to avoid paying them, but for many of us, finding the most competitive deal is possible.*

WAYS OF TACKLING DEBT. *Borrowing is a way of modern life, but you do not need to become a slave to your debts. We show you ways to unshackle yourself from debt serfdom.*

An important caveat to this book is that we assume you have chosen the worst of everything. Of course, that is highly unlikely. Nobody could manage to make a bad decision on every aspect of their personal finance; even by chance you'd end up making a few good ones.

That isn't the point, though. We assume that you have made a few crap choices and for that reason not every saving will apply to you in full, but some probably will. These will, we hope, be a big eye-opener for you, which will mean that you will put other ideas in other chapters into force and get your personal finances nice and lean.

Karl says that making a savings is the same as getting a 'raise'. That point is fair and true, so just imagine that by getting a simple book you could start to save when before you couldn't. Or that it could make a difference big enough for you to afford a holiday or to replace a car or some other big expenditure that you currently can't manage?

That's how powerful spending a little time on your personal finances can be, and because it tends to be a somewhat personal and private matter people don't go through their finances methodically on a regular basis, and that results in less than ideal outcomes.

We really hope that with this book you can get better deals, better value for money and better returns on your hard-earned money. We also believe that short and to the point is what people want, so in keeping with that belief we'll wrap up this introduction and you can get started.

01

MORTGAGE PROTECTION

TOPIC	Property
EXPECTED SAVINGS OR EARNINGS	€200
TIME REQUIRED	2 hours
LEVEL OF DIFFICULTY	● ● ● ○ ○

Some households never buy a home. Others do and pay for it in cash. Most use a mortgage to buy a home and in the process they are usually required to take out a type of life assurance called 'mortgage protection'.

What this policy does is clear the balance of the mortgage on the death of any of the policy holders. It's normally done on a 'joint life first event' basis, which means that if two people take out the policy and die simultaneously, it only pays out once and the sum is usually engineered to cover only the balance of the loan.

It does this because it's created as a 'decreasing-term' policy, which means that the amount it pays out decreases over time – just like your mortgage – and it has a set term, the same as a mortgage does. So if you take out a mortgage for €250,000 over 25 years, this policy should track it fairly closely so that if the policy holder (or holders) dies, the mortgage is cleared.

Typically, it's the cheapest type of life assurance because the risk of death increases over time, but the amount paid out decreases. As well as this, only one life is really being covered, even though many couples have this type of insurance.

WHERE THE PROBLEM LIES

Often when a person takes out a mortgage they buy their insurance from the bank. In our view this is almost always an error, for two reasons. First, the bank can only sell one policy from whomever they are getting their insurance from because banks are usually tied agents (they don't research the whole market; they have only one offering).

This lack of full market research means you might not be getting the best value. A good example of this is that AIB currently sells Irish Life policies; we'll see shortly that this can mean that you pay more than you might if you didn't buy the policy from the bank.

The second issue with buying your insurance from the bank is that sometimes the payment is mixed in with your mortgage payment and this means that if you miss mortgage payments your insurance can lapse too. This means that if a person went into arrears and then died, their loan might also not be paid off.

This is a mistake because job loss and other factors could mean that you can't meet a mortgage payment, but many people could still afford a policy that might be costing €30 a month. Both going sour at the same time is a risk you don't want to take.

HOW TO FIX IT

The fix here is to look for better value for money on this insurance. Mortgage protection isn't the most complicated product because the simple test is 'Are you alive or dead?' If you are alive, you don't have a claim; if you aren't, you do. Apart from regular terms and conditions there aren't any of the special requirements that you get with some other health-related insurances such as serious or specified illness cover.

Think about it like this. Imagine that two airlines go to the same airport you want to travel to, they offer the same in-flight services and are virtually identical except for their names. On that basis, would you willingly pay €100 more for the flight with one versus the other? If your answer is 'no', look to do the same on your mortgage protection.

THE SAVINGS EXPLAINED

A quote for a non-smoking couple, both aged 35, who are taking out a loan for €250,000 over 25 years depends on who you take out the cover with. At the time of writing, the highest price was €30.45, which was offered by Irish Life. Remember what we just mentioned about AIB?

The cheapest was €26.61, offered by New Ireland. But how do you get an even lower price? The simple answer is to use a broker who checks the whole market, because they can get you the cheapest price. Savings of €1,152 over the life of the policy aren't something you should be happy to walk away from; that's why getting a full market view is a good idea.

It doesn't stop at shopping around; brokers also control the commission within the policy and many brokers can manipulate this to get you an 'under-the-counter' offer.

One way that this can be done is by dealing with a firm that brokers for Royal London, which not only allows a price-match (this is where they sell their products at somebody else's price), but also has add-on discounts, and on top of that the broker can further discount the policy.

Using this method you could get a price of more like €22, which would represent savings of just over €100 a year or €2,500 over the term of the policy.

We have put in a higher amount of €200 savings at the top of this chapter because the explanation so far is for people who are looking at taking out a brand new policy. Many people have older policies where the prices were higher because life assurance prices have been coming down over time (recently other insurances, like car insurance, have been getting more pricey).

There is a point, depending on your age, where that trend won't benefit you, where if you tried to switch you would actually pay more (typically if you are over age 50 and have a long term left on the policy, the reason is that you are getting closer to the time where a claim might typically happen), but outside that it isn't uncommon to see people save €200 a year by moving to the lowest cost provider.

 TIME *You'll need to contact a broker, get quotes, see what the best price is, determine if you are happy with the price offered and then fill out the forms and return them. When you get the cover you'll also need to send it off to the bank. In total this will take about two hours, including your calls to the broker and the bank.*

 DIFFICULTY *This isn't completely hassle-free. It involves answering health questions, making sure you have the right amount and term, and then getting the policy issued and sent to the lender. That said, remember that in effect you could be earning the equivalent of about €100 an hour for your time!*

 SOME THINGS TO WATCH OUT FOR *Before you do this you may need to make a call to your bank to see what process is required for you to 'assign the policy', because when you take out a loan the insurance is taken out by you but owned by the bank. Most of the banks have a form that you have to fill out to assign the new policy, so get one sent out to you. There is also the issue of some banks grouping the insurance with the mortgage. These can be tricky to change, so ask what you need to do to cancel the policy you were sold and replace it with a better one.*

 USEFUL WEBSITES *Insurance brokers are listed by their association, the Professional Insurance Brokers Association, https://piba.ie.*
Some broker houses are set up just for discounts like this. Check out www.labrokers.ie or www.hello.ie.

02

RENT
A ROOM

TOPIC	Property
EXPECTED SAVINGS OR EARNINGS	Up to €14,000 a year
TIME REQUIRED	4 hours, and a new person living with you
LEVEL OF DIFFICULTY	● ● ● ● ○ (because of the new housemate)

One of the most generous tax breaks available in the entire country is the ability to get up to €14,000 a year entirely tax-free by renting out rooms in your home. This is the equivalent of going out and earning (depending on your tax band) between about €17,500 and €23,500.

This is a simple and effective way of really increasing your income and it's the same as if you saved it. Imagine being able to save a five-figure sum every year.

A word of caution: up to €14,000 is tax-free, but above that limit the entire amount becomes taxable. So if you get €14,500 in a year you pay tax on the whole lot, not just the €500 over the limit.

WHERE THE PROBLEM LIES

A lot of people don't realise that they could almost have their mortgage or rent paid for them if they rented out rooms in their house. This comes with the obvious issue of more people living with you, and some folks don't want additional people in their house, or the rooms are used by their own children, but this is an idea with big potential.

A 25-year mortgage of €200,000 with an interest rate of 4% costs just over €1,050 a month. If you were getting the full room rental amount you could be paying that mortgage off and the cost to you would be zero, your mortgage is totally covered and you'd even have money left over.

If you were renting a house for €1,200 and had two others paying €500 each per room, you'd have deeply discounted rent of only €200 a month (again, the annual amount can't go over €14,000).

In one sense, it would be a bright idea if young renters teamed up, bought together and rented out spare rooms because by doing this they could be accumulating the wealth that repayments of capital create, but we are *not* suggesting you do this because there can be other issues, so get advice if you are thinking about this.

People may not want to rent out rooms for all kinds of reasons; even older people who have spare rooms sometimes want to keep them free for when grown-up children want to visit.

HOW TO FIX IT

Put an ad online – there are lots of property sites such as Daft.ie or MyHome.ie – or contact a student exchange. If you have kids, having a person from another country live with you might even help to teach them a language. Ads in universities and further education schools also work.

You need to find the right person who you think you can get along with. Then you simply set a rent and have a chat about what is and isn't acceptable while they live with you. This isn't a 'tenancy' so you don't have to register with the Private Residential Tenancies Board.

You do have to declare the income, so log on to Revenue.ie. If your income is mainly from being employed, register for PAYE Anytime. This will allow you to file your return once a year – but the good news is that you will have a zero tax bill if you aren't getting more than €14,000.

If you are self-employed, simply add this income to your Form 11 tax return that you have to do every year anyway.

THE SAVINGS EXPLAINED

The 2015 Finance Act changed the rules on room rental. Before the Act was passed you could get up to €10,000 a year tax-free; this was increased by 20% to €12,000 for 2016 and from 2017 it's €14,000 a year. If you can rent out a room, which is a great idea if you are an empty-nester or own a home and have a spare room or travel a lot and want somebody there, the income is totally tax-free. No PRSI, no USC, nothing. It does give a slightly unfair advantage to people who own property because mortgage payments have a savings element in them, but we aren't here to set or change the rules, only to work with the rules that exist so that we can maximise your finances. The advantage to the renter is that by using the scheme they can pay lower rent than they might otherwise pay and have money to save or use elsewhere.

TIME *To advertise, talk to people and have a room ready, we figure it should take about four hours of your time. You might already know somebody and it could take far less, but the assumption here is that you will be vetting strangers.*

DIFFICULTY *Adjusting to having a new person in your home can be hard, but that doesn't make the actual task itself difficult. In many cases, roommates become lifelong friends so it can be a very positive experience too.*

THINGS TO WATCH OUT FOR *Obviously, people who are incompatible with how you live are the biggest issue. If you like the quiet life and have a party animal move in (or vice versa) it will lead to problems. Something that is in the property owner's favour is that this is not a 'tenancy'. For that reason, and often to the detriment of the roommate, they are not protected by tenancy laws and can be asked to move out rapidly.*

This should ensure that you have some comfort around who moves in, as if things aren't working out the law is on your side. While this kind of power has to be dealt with carefully and fairly, it does mean that you won't become hostage to your decision because if it doesn't work you can change it.

 USEFUL WEBSITES *If you need more information on what constitutes room rental, go to the Revenue.ie website to find out more. It's worth noting that at the time of writing, using your home for Airbnb is* not *considered room rental under this scheme. Therefore all the profits are taxable; there is no tax-free threshold. There are some other caveats – for instance, the room cannot be a granny flat or another home attached to your own house – so read the guide and make sure you are doing it right.*

Other websites you'll want to consider for renting out rooms are www. daft.ie , www.rent.ie and also www.myhome.ie.

03

MAKE EXTRA MONEY

TOPIC	Lifestyle
EXPECTED SAVINGS OR EARNINGS	€2,500
TIME REQUIRED	100–200 hours?
LEVEL OF DIFFICULTY	● ● ○ ○ ○

Would you like to have a little more money? Almost everyone would say 'Yes'. We know you agree because you bought this book. Most of us would agree that a little extra wouldn't go astray.

Often books about money only go in one direction: they either tell you to self-inflict massive austerity; or they say 'go start a business' or something. The real trick is to get the balance right. This balance means living a life you are happy with, obtaining acceptable results (in this case we mean being adequately paid for your work) in a way that best suits your life while being aware of the options available to you at any given time.

You can't work all the time – nobody can – but when you do, are you ensuring that you are getting paid for your work and paid fairly?

WHERE THE PROBLEM LIES

There are only two ways to become better off: you either spend less (and we have lots of tips about that) or you earn more. We know there is somebody smart reading this who is thinking 'What about investing? If I invest my money and it grows isn't that a way to become better off?' and the answer is yes, but to get that money to invest you'll typically have to save it and that ultimately comes from earnings.

Just to be clear about how vital earnings are, imagine Jane or Joe bought a house for €100,000 many years ago and sold it recently for €200,000 and that over the years of ownership it generated €70,000 in rental income. Leaving taxes out of it, the asset for €100,000 made them €170,000, but without earnings they would never have had it.

The reason is that (assuming they didn't inherit the house) they had to be making money to get the opportunity in the first place. So many people who advise on financial matters or who write about it miss this fundamental point – your most valuable asset in life isn't your house or your pension. It's your earning ability (which in a sense is the same as your time) because that is the key factor that goes into making it possible for you to do everything financial such as purchase a home or start saving.

Now, you can increase your earnings in a few different ways. You can go into work tomorrow and ask for a raise, or if you are self-employed you can raise your prices. These are both totally acceptable and realistic possibilities for everybody who is working.

Be prepared for your boss or customers to resist this; if they say 'no' it doesn't mean that you are wrong and not worth it, it just means that right now you don't have the necessary bargaining power or value to make the proposition too good to resist. The good news is that you can work on that.

Some people work in jobs where unions have negotiated pay scales. One of the big frustrations with that is that a high performer will be paid the same as a middle or low performer simply because they are all on the same scale. In this instance you can look for promotion (or leave that job and get a better one elsewhere), but going to the gaffer and asking for a raise definitely won't work.

In general, though, we are assuming you are doing your best already, so another way to increase your income is to work more, do a second job or turn a hobby into paid work. There is also a third choice, where you offset cost with work.

This isn't rocket science; it's more about doing the things you already do but being fairly rewarded for it.

HOW TO FIX IT

We have yet to meet a person who doesn't have some kind of skill that they could make money from. Did you ever turn on the radio and hear Charlie talking about one of the national stories that regularly hits the front pages? Well, he doesn't go on the radio for free. Granted, it isn't highly paid, but it is something and it helps him to get by. Some other people appear on radio shows and don't get paid – he just made sure he wasn't one of them. We'd encourage you to consider doing the same with whatever it is you do.

For instance, Karl plays music as a hobby. It's something he's been doing since he was a teenager. He performs a couple of nights every month and he doesn't show up and play for free or for a few pints; it's a commercial proposition. Providing entertainment can be done for free but it doesn't make sense for him to play for nothing, and nowadays it's part of his income. If you are good at music you could play gigs or teach others.

An obvious issue (in particular with some skills) is that they are under-valued. For instance, stay-at-home parents do a job that is worth tens of thousands of euro but they aren't usually remunerated for it. And in many bars musicians show up and play a trad session in exchange for a few pints, but that still amounts to a form of payment, albeit a paltry one.

What you do or how you do it matters. Everybody has different skills; what about a person who can bake, fix cars when they have problems, clean or do gardens? Is that you? Do you have any hobby or skill that is commercially viable outside whatever you already do?

If so, the chances are there are people out there who are willing to pay you to do just that. The obvious downside is that it means working more hours, so the best solution is to do something you love. If your day job happens to be something you love, that's great; spend a little more time doing it and you'll find this an easy tip. Charlie likes to write – that's what he does as a journalist, so it's natural that he'd use that skill to help write this book.

Figuring out how to do this means taking a look at your own life and seeing if there is something you like that you could do for extra money. If you can't think of anything, you could take a part-time job; there are always lots of places that need casual workers. Ideally, do something you like, because you'll be giving up precious free time, but you could also do a job you don't particularly enjoy if the goal is just to ensure you have a little more money at the end of the month rather than, as the famous country song says, 'having too much month at the end of the money'. This is trading your time in exchange for your labour; it's not really 'chasing the dream' as such, so use it as a last resort.

Don't be afraid to be creative. If you know how to do something that other people might want, then you might also know somebody who does something you want and you can trade the two off, which is also a way of saving money. Imagine a painter or decorator needs a door fixed and knows a carpenter who wants a hallway painted. They can trade off and both be better off because of it. Any difference between the value of the jobs can still be settled in money.

There is a strong chance you might already be doing something like this because so many people have large skill sets. For example, people who pursue a hobby often have the chance to get involved with running their sports team or whatever. This is usually done on a voluntary basis but then they often don't have to pay the fees or subscriptions that are normally due and in this way it offsets costs that might otherwise occur.

If you still can't think of some way of getting paid for what you know how to do, consider what you spend money on and see if you can offset the costs. You may be pleasantly surprised at some of the ideas or skills you have that you don't get paid for and what a big difference it makes when you do start to get paid fairly for them.

THE SAVINGS EXPLAINED

Let's say you decide to do something that can make you €50 a week extra by doing the activity for about four hours or thereabouts. Can't find the time? Try watching less TV, something that is normally very unproductive.

Just that extra €50 a week will keep a car taxed and insured and pay for most of your annual fuel too, or it might be two mortgage or rent payments. If you can have that kind of extra money it makes a big difference. The main thing stopping people is either that they don't want to spend their time doing whatever it is, or they haven't figured out how they can make it work.

Take a person who is very time constrained. A single working parent fits that bill perfectly. A person in that situation could do 'drop off' babysitting at their house, or they could coach or volunteer at something their child does that they would otherwise have to pay for. This kills two birds with one stone: they lower their costs; and they do an activity with their kids.

It takes some thinking, it takes some time, but extra income isn't as elusive as many people think it is. We have no way to know for sure just how big the black economy is, and we certainly are not saying you shouldn't pay your taxes. In fact, that's one thing we should stress; this extra money *is* taxable and you'll need to declare it and do tax returns based on it, but it's also well worth it.

 TIME *As mentioned, if you want to increase your income by €50 a week, then it will take time and the amount of time is dependent on what you are doing. If you have a skill you can sell at €50 per hour, then it will take one hour a week; if your hourly price is €10 then it will take five hours a week. Also, don't forget expenses – often you have to bear a cost to obtain income and that has to be factored in. For that reason you are looking at somewhere between 50 and 250 hours depending on what you do.*

 DIFFICULTY *The whole idea of increasing your income is to use something you have an ability with already. What we aren't saying is that you should spend money to go train for something which you will then do as a nixer.*

SOME THINGS TO WATCH OUT FOR *If you are making extra income, you will be liable to pay income tax on it. For this reason you should be aware of what expenses you can and cannot offset. Depending on what you do there may also be things like 'flat-rate expenses' you can claim. Also remember that if you do some jobs then you may also require insurance or licences and that a disgruntled client can turn into a legal nightmare if you cut corners when it comes to the law and regulation. A lot of jobs don't come with this caveat, so just use your common sense.*

 USEFUL WEBSITES *Try www.jobs.ie, www.gumtree.ie or local noticeboards. In order to stay tax compliant, register online for your tax returns at www.revenue.ie and ensure you are claiming your allowable expenses! Download the IT1 leaflet – income tax leaflet 1 – which tells you all the rates and allowable expenses.*

04

MOBILE PHONE CONTRACTS

TOPIC	Lifestyle
EXPECTED SAVINGS OR EARNINGS	€300
TIME REQUIRED	2 hours
LEVEL OF DIFFICULTY	●●○○○

There are more mobile phones in Ireland than there are people. There are just short of five million of the devices. We love to talk and we are big users of the data on our phones but, surprisingly, we are not keen on changing networks. This is despite the fact that you can make savings of €300 a year from ending a contract with an expensive mobile phone operator and opting for a better-value phone contract.

Last year just one in seven of us bothered to ditch our mobile phone provider for another one. That is up slightly on previous years, but it is much lower than the close to a third of people who will change motor insurer in a given year. We are often reluctant to change because we have acquired our handset from our mobile phone provider. According to the Competition and Consumer Protection Commission, the State body set up to enforce consumer protection, the savings from switching mobile phone operator are among the highest of all household bills.

WHERE THE PROBLEM LIES
Loyalty is often the reason we resist seeking a better deal. But in the case of mobile phones the sheer number of different plans, and their complexity, plays a big role too. There are hundreds of plans out there from the different operators. And comparing mobile phone plans is more complex than other industries since there are so many factors to consider. These factors include whether you make a lot of calls from your mobile to landlines or other mobiles, the time of day you call, and the network the person you are calling uses.

There are now three dominant mobile phone operators in this market. Vodafone, Three and Eir (Meteor/eMobile) are the main players. Smaller operators include Tesco and LycaMobile. Recently, Dixons Carphone launched iD Mobile, and Virgin Mobile also entered the market.

When considering switching plans you need to be clear about what kind of mobile phone user you are. Do you spend a lot of time talking on the phone, or do you prefer sending text messages? If you send a lot of messages, do you send traditional texts, or do you use tools like WhatsApp, which eats into your data allowance? How much data do you consume a month? The answer will typically be over 1GB if you consume a lot of online video and stream music. What network do the phones you contact most often use? Lots of deals include 'free calls and texts to the same network' offers that can be big savers.

Once you understand these factors, it is a case of shopping around for the most suitable plan for your needs. Do not be drawn into spending extra on unlimited plans if you are not a heavy user. Who needs unlimited texts if you never use them?

Remember that It is possible to spend €25 a month with one provider and €75 with another for exactly the same usage. Knowing what sort of mobile phone user you are will mean you can get a plan that suits you at a price that is low.

HOW TO FIX IT

You can move from one operator to another without any fuss. You can even keep your full mobile number – this is what people in the mobile phone business call 'number portability'. The main thing to be aware of when switching from one service provider to another is whether any minimum contract term applies to your existing contract, according to the telecoms regulator ComReg. If you are still in contract you will be charged cancellation fees by your existing provider if you leave before that period is up.

If you have upgraded or changed to a new package with your existing provider this can result in an extension of the minimum contract term. You should also check your existing terms and conditions to see if you are required to give 30 days' notice before leaving the current service provider. If there are no minimum term/notice period issues, all you have to do to switch is to contact the new provider and advise them that you wish to sign up to their service.

Compare the price plans on offer from the main mobile operators on the market at callcosts.ie. This site is run by ComReg. You will have to dig out a bill and enter into the website how many texts you send in a month, the amount of data you use, and your calls to landlines and to mobiles. Contact your new operator and provide your details. You can phone them, go online or call into one of their retail outlets. When you move to a new operator, you can keep your old number if you want. Your new mobile operator should complete the process for you within a few hours.

Alternatively, you can download the free app from Dublin company KillBiller (www.killbiller.com). This app burrows into your phone and assesses your phone usage. It then tells you what you would spend on all available plans, with your own network or another operator. It can also put you in touch with the mobile operator of your chosen plan, who can facilitate a switch.

And remember that you can break out of your mobile phone contract when the provider increases their prices, as this is considered a change in the terms and conditions of the contract. There will be no penalty if you choose this time to move to another operator.

There is no need to notify your existing provider if you are out of contract, either because the contract term is up, or there has been a price rise. Once your number has moved over to the new network your current provider will generate your last bill and this will be sent to you either by post or email.

THE SAVINGS EXPLAINED

Most of the plans that are priced between €25 and €35 a month will meet the needs of most mobile users. If you are on an old plan you could be paying a multiple of these amounts.

Whether you pay as you use your phone (top-up or pay as you go) or monthly (billpay), there will be an option that is likely to save you money. Average phone users can get plans for as little as €20 a month. Big data users can usually find a plan that will cost no more than €30 a month, while those into texting can opt for a plan that gives a generous allowance to those who like to send texts for as little as €30 a month.

 TIME *You will need to dig out your bill from your mobile provider. This is your starting point when researching what other plans are out there and the value they offer. You will need to enter details about your call activity and data use on comparison site callcosts.ie. You will then need to check that you are free to move (not locked into a contract). Then contact your chosen operator. In all, your research should take about an hour, and everything else another half an hour.*

 DIFFICULTY *Some work is involved, but the savings can be big.*

 SOME THINGS TO WATCH OUT FOR *You may be locked into a one-year contract, or even an 18-month one, with your existing provider. There will be penalties for exiting the contract early, which will negate any savings from switching. If you recently upgraded your phone, that may have involved extending your current contract. So make sure you are out*

of contract before considering switching. If you are still in a contract, you might save by moving to a different plan with your existing operator. If you do switch to a different operator, remember to write to your bank to cancel any direct debit with the old provider.

 USEFUL WEBSITES *The regulator's site is at www.callcosts.ie. It's also worth looking at www.killbiller.com.*

05

HEALTH
INSURANCE

TOPIC	Medical expenses
EXPECTED SAVINGS OR EARNINGS	€360
TIME REQUIRED	4 hours
LEVEL OF DIFFICULTY	● ● ● ● ○

The cost of health insurance is constantly rising. Higher levels of claims and more frequent claims, costs imposed by the State and medical inflation all get blamed. The expectation now is that we are going to get price hikes twice a year from insurers. Yet despite this, almost half the population has a private health insurance policy. And despite the financial turmoil the country has experienced in the last decade the number of people with health insurance has remained remarkably high.

OK   1K   2K   3K   4K   5K   6K   7K   8K   9K   10K   11K   12K

Access to a consultant without having to endure being put on long and lengthening waiting lists, and the option to be treated in a private hospital or in a private or semi-private room in a public hospital are the big pluses of having medical insurance.

The good news is that with three providers in the market and hundreds of different health plans, there is great value to be had if you know where to look. Here we offer a guide to some simple tactics to help you find the best-value option for you or your family that will still give you excellent overall cover but at the best price possible.

Typically, the best deals are offered to corporate clients or company-paid group schemes, but anyone can join these so-called corporate plans. These typically represent the best value in the market for those happy with semi-private cover and happy to take on a small excess per admission to private hospitals only.

WHERE THE PROBLEM LIES

Continuing and substantial price increases, and constant changes to what is covered in plans, means that anyone who has not changed health insurance plan in the last two years is highly likely to be overpaying. Only 6% of households switched health insurance provider in 2016, according to research conducted for the Competition and Consumer Protection Commission, the State body that protects consumers. Surprisingly, the same research found that 37% of people with health cover never bothered to check if they could get better value by switching to a different plan with their current provider, or to another insurer.

Misplaced loyalty, inertia and a fear of the hassle involved in switching are all contributing to a situation where too few people are gaining switcher savings. And the savings are considerable – some €360 a year is possible, according to the State consumer body.

Some people fear that if they move to another provider they will lose out. They mistakenly feel they have built up credits with their current insurer and will have those removed if they move. But remember, health insurance legislation protects you when switching – you must get full credit for any time insured with another insurer(s). Therefore, if you have already served your waiting periods, you do not have to do so again just because you have swapped provider.

Another problem is that people get talked out of moving if they first contact their existing insurer.

The good news is that tax relief is available on the first €1,000 for each adult and €500 for every child's premium at 20%. This is done at source, so the prices you are quoted already include it.

HOW TO FIX IT

Like most products, there are no rewards for loyalty when you have health insurance. This means you can switch policy, or insurance provider, every year. You can even do this from a hospital bed while receiving treatment as long as you have come to the end of your one-year contract. If you are doing that, do make sure that the new plan covers the hospital, consultant and procedure you are undertaking.

The first thing to do is to set a budget. Decide how much you can afford to spend to cover all the family. It is worth remembering that the level of cover you will get for low-priced plans is generally not worth buying. This means that you need to be spending at least €800 per adult for decent cover.

Take your time. Health insurance is mind-bogglingly complicated, with three providers and hundreds of different plans. You could go to a broker to do the work for you. Some charge a fee, others get a commission from insurers, but all will make the process easier.

If you decide to do the work yourself, you will need to set aside at least half a day to research different plans, and their prices. Use the website of the Health Insurance Authority, the State regulatory body for the sector, at www.hia.ie. This site will allow you to compare your current plan with others that offer similar benefits.

Another approach is to telephone your current provider, and the others in the market, and ask insurance companies: 'What is your very best plan for my budget? And please include all your corporate plans.' They will then be obliged to search through all their products. You should be able to make savings of €360 for two adults, two children (aged 7 and 4) on a low-range plan (semi-private in public hospital cover).

THE SAVINGS EXPLAINED

A family of two adults and two children should be able to get a good level of cover for €2,500 a year. If you have been on the same plan for a number of years the chances are you are paying too much as insurers have been pushing up premiums and lowering benefits on older plans. It is worth considering insuring different family members on different plans. The cheaper plans should be reserved for kids and teens or adults with good workplace illness benefits, and look out for special offers that insure kids for less, or free. You may want to go further and consider whether it is worth having children covered at all. There are no private hospitals or beds in Ireland for children, so insuring them may be a waste of money.

It is worth deciding what type of cover you need. Is a private room vital or do you mind sharing? This element will make a huge difference in cost. Do you want outpatient benefits, like refund of GP fees? Are you currently receiving treatment?

A good way to save money is to take on an excess. This is one of the best tactics open to all consumers to slash your costs. A major fear that consumers have is that the excess is per night, which is not the case. On most plans, the excess is per admission or per claim (including day-case claims) and it only applies to private hospitals. When taking on an excess, you must consider the worst-case scenario, i.e. if I need to be admitted multiple times during the year, could I afford to pay an excess of anything from €50 to €150 per admission each time? If you are attending a public hospital in a private capacity, no excess applies. In most cases, the excesses will not be applied at all for cancer-related day-case treatments such as chemotherapy or radiotherapy.

If you have never had health cover before, a waiting period of five years applies for pre-existing conditions. Some insurers will reduce this, but you have to ask.

 TIME *Health insurance is a complicated product. You do not want to end up being denied treatment because you have cut your level of benefits too much in a bid to save money. So you will need time to research the plans. If you use a broker, much of this legwork will be done for you. But you will still need to set aside time to brief the broker and then assess the choices offered to you. All this is likely to take at least four hours, but you may need to allow more time than that.*

DIFFICULTY *There is no getting away from the fact that seeking out better-value health insurance is not an easy task. Maybe that is why 32% of people told the researchers commissioned by the Competition and Consumer Protection Commission that they have never checked to see if they could get a better deal on their health cover.*

 SOME THINGS TO WATCH OUT FOR *Look out for special offers. From time to time all insurers offer discounts for switchers. Corporate plans are designed by insurers for their big clients who often pay for their employees' cover. These corporate plans tend to have higher levels of benefits and are often better value. By law, these plans must be made available to everyone. However, the names are deliberately obscure.*

 USEFUL WEBSITES *Check out the Health Insurance Authority at www. hia.ie. It's also worth looking up the website of leading health insurance broker Dermot Goode at www.totalhealthcover.ie.*

06

TAX
REFUNDS

TOPIC	Tax breaks
EXPECTED SAVINGS OR EARNINGS	€900
TIME REQUIRED	4 hours
LEVEL OF DIFFICULTY	● ● ● ○ ○

The average household is estimated to be missing out on around €880 a year in tax refunds. Many people are failing to claim tax refunds and avail of tax breaks. According to tax practitioners, we are getting better at claiming what is ours from the Revenue Commissioners, but we are still not claiming everything that is owed to us. We need to get into a habit every year of claiming what is due to us in tax refunds. After all, it is our money.

Tax efficiency has become more commonplace among the Irish public, but there are still thousands of people who will leave millions of euro with the taxman this year – don't be one of them.

This is especially important as austerity budgets have left a legacy of people paying more in taxes and charges, stealth and otherwise, than ever before. Pay cuts and job losses have also eaten into earnings for the average household.

WHERE THE PROBLEM LIES

Most people don't know that they are entitled to a refund of some of the tax they paid in the previous year. They may also have a justifiable fear of the taxman. They worry that interacting with Revenue will mean only one thing – that they will end up paying more tax. But you have nothing to fear from the tax authorities if you are honest, and lots to gain if you are failing to claim all your reliefs and allowances. The list of tax refunds for PAYE (pay as you earn) employees has narrowed considerably in the last few years, but you can still claim money back. Just because your employer automatically deducts tax every week or month does not mean that you can't get a portion of it back at the end of the year.

Many people are unaware that you can go back as far as four years. But once the four-year deadline passes you are locked out of getting a refund. This means you could lose out on hundreds, even thousands, of euros.

Taxpayers may be put off by the hassle involved in getting refunds, and may be reluctant to have any dealings with the Revenue Commissioners, but it is worth noting that little effort is required. And it is not the case that Revenue officials deliberately make it difficult to reclaim tax. The opposite is actually the case. You can even use your mobile phone to make a claim. So why leave the money with the taxman?

HOW TO FIX IT

You will need to dig out your PPS (personal public service) number, collect receipts, sign a form or two, wait two to six weeks, and you should get money back off the taxman. Alternatively, you can claim tax refunds online or on your mobile phone.

In some cases you can get a tax refund for specific expenses, for example medical expenses or mortgage interest. The value of a tax allowance will depend on whether it is allowed at the highest rate of income tax that you pay or is restricted to the standard 20% rate. In simple terms this means that if you have a claim for €100 and you pay tax at 40% you can claim back €40. If the highest rate of tax you pay is 20%, or the relief is restricted to the standard rate, the claim of €100 will reduce your tax by €20.

THE SAVINGS EXPLAINED

One of the easiest things to make a claim on is medical expenses. Relief can be claimed as a tax credit for un-reimbursed medical expenses incurred on your own behalf or for others. You don't have to be related to any other individual whose expenses you might be paying. However, the relief cannot be claimed unless you have remembered to keep all your receipts. Expenses qualifying for relief would include the cost of doctors' and consultants' fees, prescription medicines, physiotherapy and routine maternity care. The tax credit is 20% of the amount of medical expenses which have not been reimbursed by a health insurer. It's possible to claim this credit in several ways – on your tax return, by submitting form MED 1 or by using Revenue's web-based PAYE Anytime service.

The fact that employees are allowed flat-rate expenses is often missed out on. Revenue has arrangements in place to grant flat-rate expenses for employees working in a range of activities.

Nurses, optometrists, panel beaters, grooms, musicians, journalists and air crew, to name just a few, may claim fixed expenses provided certain conditions are met. The easiest way to check if you are eligible is to go onto the Revenue website at www.revenue.ie and search for 'List of Flat-Rate Schedule E Expenses'. In limited circumstances, other expenses of employment can be claimed if you run them up 'wholly, exclusively and necessarily', as the rule puts it. But this is very difficult to establish to Revenue's satisfaction. The costs of travelling to and from work are never allowed if you're an employee. That's partly why there are special allowances for bikes and travel passes.

It's worth noting that tuition fees for third-level courses will qualify for income tax relief at the standard rate of tax on most full-time and part-time courses. The relief is only available on the excess over €3,000 for full-time courses, and €1,500 for part-time courses. In general, this has the effect of allowing relief on the tuition fees on the second or later children. The taxpayer has the option of deciding which year to make the claim, i.e. either in the year of payment or the year of commencement of the course.

Many people wrongly believe that the Home Carer Tax Credit is for those caring for other people's children, the elderly or disabled people. They don't realise that it can be claimed where any housewife or house-husband works in the home, caring for their own children. Having been increased recently to €1,100, this credit is more valuable than ever. It is available to any jointly assessed couple with one or more children, where the non-assessable spouse has income of less than €7,200 in 2017.

 TIME *Claiming your medical expenses will take an hour or two. Gathering up your expenses and adding them together will take most of the effort. The MED 1 form will take 20 minutes to fill out. When it comes to flat-rate expenses it is a case of applying to Revenue for the one that relates to your employment. To claim the tuition fees relief, complete the relevant claim form (available as a PDF, 214KB) and forward it to your Revenue office. Allow four hours in total.*

 DIFFICULTY *Claiming money off the Revenue Commissioners is less complicated than you might think. When you have done it once, it becomes even easier next time.*

 SOME THINGS TO WATCH OUT FOR *People sometimes make the mistake of assuming Revenue have all the correct and relevant data on them. If a spouse or partner is claiming social welfare they assume the tax officials know that, or they assume the tax authorities know they have a medical card. Government departments do not share as much information as we think. It is worth your while ensuring that Revenue has the correct details on your tax affairs.*

 USEFUL WEBSITES *Revenue – www.revenue.ie – and www.citizensinformation.ie contain a raft of information.*

07

QUIT SMOKING

TOPIC	Lifestyle
EXPECTED SAVINGS OR EARNINGS	€3,650
TIME REQUIRED	Lifetime (but really just a few weeks to get started)
LEVEL OF DIFFICULTY	● ● ● ● ●

One of the most stupid things you can do for your health and wealth is to smoke. Both Charlie and Karl are ex-smokers (the worst type of anti-smoker), and both know too well that it's a terrible choice financially.

Paying about a tenner a day to shorten your life is pointless and a drain on your finances. If you are a smoker, giving up ought to be high on your 'to do' list and it's very high on our money-saving tips list too! In fact, when it comes to discretionary non-essential consumables (and being addicted doesn't mean it isn't a 'discretionary non-essential'), this ranks as one of the biggest items you'll find on many people's list.

Apart from being a nasty habit it's an inconvenience and more and more places are smoke-free, so why not give it a try? Karl was a heavy smoker and says that in retrospect the freedom of not being a slave to tobacco is great.

Too many people quit successfully for this to not be considered. It may not be that easy, and it's going to change many aspects of your life. Many smokers tie the habit into their lives to such an extent that it almost becomes hard-wired into their existence.

If you are an ex-smoker or current smoker you'll know what we mean when we talk about the way that smoking becomes part of having a drink or a coffee, or a way to finish a meal.

That's why the timeline on this one is 'a lifetime', and the level of difficulty is high. Many people try and fail, but we are going to assume you don't fail and that you make huge savings.

WHERE THE PROBLEM LIES

Smoking is addictive. If it wasn't addictive, people probably wouldn't smoke every day. There are smokers who say they enjoy it, but none of them would willingly throw away thousands of euros a year, so think about it like this: if you didn't smoke you could buy a new car. By 'new' of course we mean a fairly new second-hand car, but don't let that change the view of how big a deal this can be. It's the difference between having a family holiday or not; it's the difference between having savings or a nest egg; and at the root of it, due to the health risks, it is quite literally the difference between life and death.

A big part of the problem is getting started. Procrastination is the enemy, but not being mentally ready is just as bad, so we suggest you figure out what approach you'll use.

Karl swears that Alan Carr's 'easy way' books helped him. You could try that or visit some of the websites we list at the end of this chapter.

HOW TO FIX IT

Never smoke another cigarette or tobacco product again for the rest of your life. It's so incredibly simple! If only every tip we had was worth so much money and so utterly easy to understand.

The execution of the plan is the tricky bit. Giving up and never touching another smoke can be tough, but it's worth it. One idea that might be worth trying is to put €10 in a jar every day you don't smoke, as if you were still paying for cigarettes, and then see how much you have after a few weeks. Smoking is incredibly expensive, it's an inconvenience and it's worth never doing it again.

There are whole industries around the 'quit smoking' process, so do whatever works for you. It may take a few attempts, you might be one of the lucky ones who finds it fairly easy. Better yet, you might not be a smoker at all and this tip won't even apply to you (the best choice of all!).

THE SAVINGS EXPLAINED

Assuming you smoke 20 a day and you are paying about €10 a day, you're spending €3,650 a year. Obviously this strips out any times when you might smoke more than a pack (such as nights out). If you smoke less, just do the sums – if you smoke half a pack the savings will be half – but no matter what you smoke, the savings from quitting are 100% worth it.

The savings that we can't easily account for are discussed later in the book when we look at some of the effects of health on your wealth. The fact that smokers have a 50% chance of getting cancer directly as a result of their habit ought to be a sufficient incentive to quit.

Ask any previously heavy smoker and they may tell you that in the end you spend the money elsewhere, but even if that is the case, it's a better choice than spending it in order to invest in your own early death. The same ex-smoker will probably tell you that after a while, far from missing the smokes, you start to hate them, and even feel sorry for people who are still stuck in the cycle of addiction they put you through.

TIME *The time needed to quit smoking is about one second – the moment you take your last inhalation of life-reducing smoke and breathe it out you can become a 'non-smoker'. The tricky thing is implementing the change for the rest of your life. As an ex-smoker, Karl can attest to the value and importance of doing this, as it vastly improves your health, the expected time you have on earth and the quality of life you lead as well as being worth a lot of money. So in some respects this is both a very short-term and very long-term commitment. The short term is becoming an ex-smoker; the long term is keeping it that way.*

 DIFFICULTY *Clearly, conquering an addiction has to rank fairly high on the 'difficulty' spectrum. We believe that if it was simple to quit smoking we would have far fewer smokers nationally than we do. If it was easy there would be no tobacco market, and despite the known health risks we have new smokers coming on-stream every year. That said, anything worth doing is never easy and the benefits of becoming a non-smoker versus staying a smoker are so extreme that the challenge is worth it.*

 SOME THINGS TO WATCH OUT FOR *Going back is easy. One of your authors (OK, it was Karl) was so adamant that they had quit for good that to show off they smoked a cigarette at a party and were instantly re-hooked and had to go through the difficult path of stopping AGAIN just because they were not aware of how insidious a habit it can be.*

Another thing to be wary of is replacing one bad habit with another. In the early days you might want to eat some sweets or some other comfort food to help get through the cravings, which is fine, but if it becomes an embedded habit then you'll see the weight pile on. A lot of people do gain a few pounds when quitting cigarettes – just be aware of the difference between a short-term crutch and a long-term habit.

 USEFUL WEBSITES *www.quit.ie, www.cancer.ie*

08

COMPOSTING

TOPIC	Household spending
EXPECTED SAVINGS OR EARNINGS	€100
TIME REQUIRED	4 hours
LEVEL OF DIFFICULTY	● ● ● ○ ○

Composting is not just a sensible idea, it's also a money-saving tip. We are going to approach this in two stages: building a dirt-cheap composter; then estimating how much you can save by using it. According to the European Commission, Ireland generates the fourth highest waste per person in the EU – 623kg per person. How do you chop that down and save on bin fees? Easy: reduce, reuse and recycle, the 'Three Rs'. Composting can cut down on a huge amount of waste. Paper, plastic and bottle recycling also help a lot. The government has jacked up the landfill levy, too, which means that getting rid of rubbish is even more expensive. If you made a genuine effort to segregate waste and got a small composter while using the recycling and organic waste bins more often it wouldn't be long before you'd be saving money.

WHERE THE PROBLEM LIES

It's easy to just throw everything away, but remember that when you do that you are doing the equivalent of just throwing your money away. The issue is that it's usually done in such small amounts that you don't notice it happening and something may not seem heavy when you put it in the bin but is the bin light when you go to lift it?

HOW TO FIX IT

Go to a building site, a builders' merchants or a garden centre and ask them if they have any pallets. They don't have to be in perfect nick, just not totally destroyed. You are going to nail four of them together to make them into the four walls of a composter. For the roof of it you can use any spare timber or a cheap sheet of plywood. Use any spare gloss paint you have in the house or in a hardware shop buy whatever is cheapest – often certain colours or small pot sizes are sold off cheaply – and paint the outside of your composter.

Unless you are totally un-handy this should be easy enough; but you could always ask whomever in your family is handy to help you out. It's also worth cutting a door into the bottom of the front wall of your composter so you can scoop it out when it's made rather than having to dig down through it to reach the compost. This composter is going to be about 4ft by 4ft in size. If you live in an apartment this won't work, but for anybody in a rural area or a housing estate some variation of it will be possible.

There are composters suitable for balconies in apartments, but they normally have to be bought.

THE SAVINGS EXPLAINED

You can compost all sorts of things that people often don't put in: grass cuttings (but too much isn't good), leaves, whatever you might sweep up off patios or paths, and newspapers. Raw vegetable peelings or leftover raw vegetables can go in too. Cooked food can't go in, but composting can take a huge amount of waste, which breaks down into a fine material that can be used as nutrient-rich fertiliser.

Composting is also a good way to throw out less – green and brown bins are 'underfed' in many households. Almost everybody I have ever met (including your authors) doesn't reduce waste by composting as much as they could. This means that you are paying more for the convenience of being a little lazy and hurting the environment by not recycling. That makes no sense, so make the effort.

Savings of €2 a week, in the region of €100 a year, are very achievable. This saving is found by putting out the main bin less. If you have an organic waste bin, that can help cut back costs too as it takes all your cooked food leftovers. The composter takes all the things that are biodegradable and the recycling bin can take the rest. The only things that need to go into your most expensive bin are whatever can't go elsewhere. If you approach it like that you'll be saving money in no time.

 TIME *It takes about the same time to compost something as it does to throw it out, some segregation of waste is required, but if you are making a better environmental choice and saving money at the same time it's a no-brainer.*

 DIFFICULTY *Low to none, a change of habit is all it takes, if you have something you are going to throw out anyway then it's just making sure you throw it out into the right place.*

 THINGS TO WATCH OUT FOR *Our waste food can become the best laid out meal for various vermin species, so keep an eye out for evidence of rats, also remember that your compost needs variety, too much of only one thing can make it less usable, and lastly, never compost cooked foods or any meats, they will rot, but it won't do your compost (or the smell in the area) any good.*

 USEFUL WEBSITES *www.stopfoodwaste.ie, https://eartheasy.com*

09
BUY
IN BULK

TOPIC	Household spending
EXPECTED SAVINGS OR EARNINGS	€500
TIME REQUIRED	1 hour
LEVEL OF DIFFICULTY	● ○ ○ ○ ○

There are some things in life that you will never stop doing, such as using loo roll after going to the toilet. You'll probably also continue to brush your teeth, wash your hair, do laundry and clean dishes.

The things you use for all this typically have no 'best before' date; some products are obliged to display one, even though it hardly matters. If the idea of using out-of-date soap bothers you, don't buy a load of it. For other things there are key times when you can save and for that reason there are times when you should bulk buy them.

WHERE THE PROBLEM LIES

Often there are 50% off or 'two-for-one' deals on things you will continue to use for ever. The makers of many premium products often do discounted deals to gain customers and then the prices go up again. A good starting point is to compare the ingredients and the order they appear in for 'store brand' and 'premium brand'; if they are the same, the two products are probably close to like-for-like. Even the own-label products go on sale from time to time.

For this reason it's a mistake to pass them by because we usually end up buying the full-price ones a short time later.

Imagine if you could rig it so that you get that same deal on everything that is half price for the whole year. If you bulk buy the best deals around, it almost works out that way.

HOW TO FIX IT

We won't often tell you to splurge in order to save, but in this instance it makes sense. If you see your favourite shampoo, shower gel, soap, dishwasher tabs, shaving gel, razors, toilet paper or other products on sale for 50% off or 'two for one', fill your basket with them.

This does mean that you'll need somewhere to put them, which can be an issue if you don't have much storage space, but we'll assume that you only choose to do this with something bulky like toilet paper.

An interesting bit of research carried out in the USA, called 'frugality is hard to afford', looked at household wealth and the amount of money people paid for toilet paper. The researchers found that the less well off you are, the more you paid for toilet paper!

The reason this happens is because the people who need discounts the most are usually the least well placed to use them. They face a 'poverty penalty'. They have to buy in small quantities and have little inventory at home and can't wait until a sale presents itself to purchase again. You don't need to be the same – a strategic purchase or two can fix this.

THE SAVINGS EXPLAINED

According to the Insolvency Service of Ireland, a person has about €35 a month to spend on toiletries (this is the minimum – many people spend much more). If you could save half of that by only buying when big discounts apply (as they regularly do), you'd save about €18 a month, which for a whole year is €216. if you have a partner and two kids that figure could more than double, which is where our €500 savings by bulk buying estimate comes from.

This could also be on the lower side of what is possible because things like washing-up liquid and dishwasher tablets are not 'toiletries'.

 TIME *Given you have to buy these things anyway, it takes virtually no time at all to buy something in bulk when you see a good deal on it. In fact, it might save some time because you won't run out of something and have to keep replacing it.*

 DIFFICULTY *The main issue is being able to afford to buy in bulk. The idea is good but you have to have the cash on hand to avail of bulk discounts and that isn't always an easy thing to do.*

 SOME THINGS TO WATCH OUT FOR *Using more of something because you have a lot of it is a risk. If you have lots of paper towels you may start to use them at times you wouldn't have used them before. The other thing to watch out for is 'false value'. Often, retailers will say something is 'on sale', but what has really happened is that they put an unusually high price on the item in the past and have now discounted it to sell a lot of it – but it's still selling at a price that is above the basic value. If you want an example of this, look at dishwasher tablets the next time you are in a shop as they often go through big price fluctuations.*

 USEFUL WEBSITES *If you do your shopping online, check the discounts available. If you do your shopping in person, just keep your eyes peeled.*

10

ENERGY

TOPIC	Household spending
EXPECTED SAVINGS OR EARNINGS	€320
TIME REQUIRED	2 hours
LEVEL OF DIFFICULTY	● ● ● ○ ○

Value hunters have long known about the benefits of moving their custom from one electricity supplier and one gas supplier to others. We are the keenest energy switchers in Europe, according to comparison data from the Commission for Energy Regulation. Despite that, most people do not switch and so are losing out on the best deals. The majority of those who have gone to the trouble of switching to cheaper gas and electricity suppliers are likely to have done it at least once in the last three or four years. But to keep benefiting from the best prices you have to switch again at the end of the discounted period. Alternatively, contact your existing supplier and ask for a better deal when the one-year deal you signed up to is finished.

The good news is that an energy provider is one of the easiest of all services to switch. There is no interruption to your supply and no one needs to visit your home to flick switches or install any new equipment. In fact, you can do it all over the phone. This makes it all the more exasperating that fewer than four out of five households do not switch regularly, and many of these have never switched at all. That inertia is costing consumers a packet and making it easy for energy suppliers to make money in this market.

WHERE THE PROBLEM LIES

There are eight electricity suppliers to homes in this country, and five gas suppliers. Electricity suppliers include the ESB's Electric Ireland, Bord Gáis, SSE Airtricity, Energia, Panda Power, PrePayPower and Pinergy, and among the gas suppliers are Electric Ireland, Bord Gáis, Energia and Flogas.

Despite the large number of competing suppliers, we pay among the highest prices for electricity in Europe. Even higher prices are charged to those who do not switch to get better deals. There are around 1.6 million households in the country and at least half have remained (foolishly) loyal to their electricity and gas suppliers over the past five years. Suppliers retain the best deals for switchers in a bid to build their market share. When they are challenged on why they are not lowering their prices they can always usefully point to the offers they have for those willing to switch. If the rest are not going to move, then why offer them a deal?

The reluctance to switch is due to inertia, the requirement to sign up for direct debits and agree to electronic billing to get the best discount rates, and a reluctance among older people and social welfare recipients to move from Electric Ireland, which automatically applies allowances to bills under the Household Benefits Package paid for by the Department of Social Protection.

HOW TO FIX IT

Seek out the keenest deals, rates and discounts, by logging on to accredited gas and electricity price comparison and switching services like Bonkers.ie or Switcher.ie. These sites have to meet strict criteria to gain their accreditation from the Commission for Energy Regulator as energy price comparison sites. They offer very easy comparisons when you fill in all the relevant information online about your average usage, including information about extra discounts if you are prepared to opt for direct debit payments and online billing.

To change your electricity supplier, you will need your MPRN (meter point reference number). This meter reference number is unique to your home and you can find it at the top of your electricity bill. When it comes to switching gas suppliers, you will need the GPRN (gas point reference number), which is printed on your gas bill.

When you switch, you will need to provide meter readings. This is so that your new supplier will know when to start billing and your old supplier will know when to stop. Taking readings yourself is best, but if you cannot do this, provide the readings from the last bill.

It normally takes up to four weeks for the switch, but it is often done much more quickly than this, and there will be no interruption in your supply. You should get a closing statement based on your meter reading and once you have paid that, all your bills will come from your new supplier. You will know when the switch has been effected when you get a welcome pack from your new supplier.

THE SAVINGS EXPLAINED

Households that part company with the most expensive providers of electricity and gas to the cheapest in the market will save €360 over the course of a year, according to the Commission for Energy Regulation. Along with price discounts, suppliers also offer cash-back deals, loyalty card points to be redeemed in supermarkets, and deals on boiler servicing.

Cash-back deals are usually attached to offers that involve discounts. The cash is paid out in the form of a bill credit, which customers will receive on their first or second bill. Often these cash-back offers range from €50 to €175, depending on the provider.

Suppliers of both gas and electricity offer what they call 'dual-fuel' discounts if you sign up to them as your sole supplier. However, the cheapest deal on gas and electricity is often to be found by getting your fuels from separate suppliers, according to both Bonkers.ie and Switcher.ie.

TIME *You should be able to switch one service, such as electricity, in half an hour. The same applies again if you are switching both services. However, it might be best to allow two hours in case you are left hanging on the phone.*

 DIFFICULTY *Swapping one energy supplier for another is the easiest household service to switch.*

 SOME THINGS TO WATCH OUT FOR *The majority of new customer energy discounts expire after a year. When your discount ends you are moved to your energy supplier's standard unit rates. Typically these are the most expensive. However, you are often not told by your supplier that the discount period has ended. This means it is worth making a note on a calendar, or in the calendar app on your smartphone, to remind you at least a week before the discount period ends so you have time to seek out a new offer. Also worth noting is that to get the best deals you will need to agree to pay by direct debit from your bank account, and accept electronic billing. If you try to switch but have not ended the fixed-term contact, you are likely to be charged an exit penalty. This will likely negate any benefit of switching. Another thing to consider is whether you owe money to your existing supplier. Energy suppliers are allowed to flag to each other if a consumer is in arrears on their energy bill and are likely to refuse the switcher custom of someone with an unpaid bill.*

 USEFUL WEBSITES *Your best bet is to go to www.bonkers.ie and www. switcher.ie. Both of these comparison websites are accredited by the Commission for Energy Regulation, so you can expect honest and independent information on prices and deals from the various energy companies. The websites of each energy supplier are worth trying, but be careful to properly survey the entire market.*

11
BEAT
THE BANK

TOPIC	Banking
EXPECTED SAVINGS OR EARNINGS	€160
TIME REQUIRED	2 days
LEVEL OF DIFFICULTY	● ● ● ○ ○

Day-to-day banking has become expensive for consumers. Some people are now paying their bank €160 a year for the use of a current account, and that does not include overdraft interest charges. Irish people are some of the worst when it comes to demanding value for money – if we took action as often as we are willing to complain about something, we'd live in a far better-served economy.

One area where this is obvious in is how we bank. Research that was done back in the early 2000s showed that people are more likely to leave their spouse than leave their bank (on the current account, day-to-day banking side of things). This is an indictment against better value.

The days of banks competing with each other to offer fee-free banking and other inducements to entice people to bank with them are long gone. Instead, incessant increases in the fees and charges banks levy for using a current account seem to have become the norm. The insidious introduction of charges for a service that was formerly free has really angered people, as it comes after the public was forced to pump €64bn into the domestic banks to bail them out.

Many banks impose transaction and maintenance fees when it comes to current accounts, so you could be paying more than you have to pay. At the same time, many banks have pulled back on the products and services they offer to the public – Bank of Ireland's restrictions on over-the-counter cash withdrawals and lodgements is one such example.

Any banks that have tried to gain market share in day-to-day banking are often recycling the same customers who initially left some other big bank to begin with. These nomadic clients are always hunting for good value; and you should be too because it pays to pay less when it comes to banking.

WHERE THE PROBLEM LIES

You can avoid fees, especially if you are a pensioner, while banks do have options for avoiding paying transaction fees and maintenance charges, but often these come with strict terms and conditions that you must meet in order to avoid paying dearly.

Banks rely on the apathy of their customers to allow them to keep imposing more charges and fees. They know most Irish people still bank with the first institution they ever opened an account with when they made their first Holy Communion. They know too that if they get your Communion money they probably have you for life.

They also know that the place where you have your current account is also the most likely place you will go to get the likes of a more profitable proposition such as a mortgage and other insurance products; furthermore, they don't have to let you know about other better deals on the market, so they have a captive audience.

There are two big enemies of finding value with current accounts (and many money-saving tips). The first is inertia – people often don't realise they are spending as much as they are on banking. The second is the perceived hassle of opening an account. If you ask anybody who did it lately, they'll tell you that the idea that it's easy is more about marketing than fact, but at least one bank has just changed all of that.

We'll tell you about that in a minute, but for now just remember that if you add up the many times you pay for different things it's no surprise to see that anything above zero is too much.

Why? Because usually banks are using things like Visa Debit and every time you use their card to pay for something they are making money on it anyway. Then there are things like ATM fees which, when applied, are usually 25–35c per use; account fees; fees for having an overdraft even if you don't use it and more fees if you do; and special 'referral fees' if you inadvertently go overdrawn without having an authorised overdraft.

In the past you used to get an overdraft and it was sanctioned for the foreseeable future; now they're reviewed every year, which often means €25 to set it up and €25 at every annual renewal. The interest payable is zero in most cases.

There are fees for making payments, fees for contactless payments, commissions for withdrawing money abroad, for sending money abroad, fees for lodging a cheque, and even fees for setting up a standing order.

Suffice to say, people often don't realise just how much they are spending on banking; and taking a look at this and adding it up to an annual cost can be quite an eye-opener.

HOW TO FIX IT

Thousands of people took to the streets to protest over water charges. But there is no need to protest publicly to effect change when it comes to bank charges. If a few thousand people switched bank accounts that would have a profound impact on banks and force the high-charging ones to cut their current account fees.

The first thing to check out is if you can still get free banking from your institution. Free banking is usually available in some guise in most banks, although it can be very difficult, and expensive, to comply with the conditions. For example, if you keep a credit balance of €2,500 at all times in your AIB current account you will not be charged fees. However, this figure is beyond most people.

If you are 66 or older Bank of Ireland allows you avoid quarterly current account transaction fees. There is also no overdraft facility fee and free contactless payments.

AIB's Advantage Account gives the 66-plus generation free banking and foreign exchange services. Ulster Bank will still allow you to get free banking once you turn 60, as do KBC and Permanent TSB.

If you cannot avail of fee-free banking from your bank, your best bet is to switch. The Central Bank's Switching Code of Conduct dictates that a bank must have a new account up and running in ten working days. This is a statutory code, meaning that all providers offering current accounts must comply with it. The bank must assist you in moving direct debits/standing orders in a timely fashion.

Pick a new bank and ask for their 'switching pack'. The first thing to do is to agree a switching date. This should be a day when there is little activity in your account. In other words, not the day your mortgage or another big bill is due out of your account.

You will be given the option to keep your old account or to close it. You must let your new bank know before you switch. If you keep your old account open you may have to pay charges on this account, and stamp duty on your cards, even if you no longer use it. If you decide to close your old account, return any unused cheques for your old account to your old bank to receive a refund of government stamp duty, the Competition and Consumer Protection Commission advises.

If you are paid directly into your bank account, you must give your new bank account details to your employer and anyone else who pays money into your bank account. Your new bank cannot do this for you. You will need to inform your employer of the new bank details.

If you have an existing overdraft, then you will have to negotiate its terms with your new bank. You are not automatically entitled to move it.

The new bank may carry out a credit check. Provide your new bank with proof of identity and confirm whether you need a cheque book, debit card and credit card. Complete an 'account transfer form'. This tells your new bank about direct debits and standing orders, which they will liaise with your old bank to switch across. The balance of funds in your old account will also be moved. Your new account will be up and running within ten days of the switching date you selected.

Another idea, if you don't want to put up with onerous rules and you are not over the age of 66, is to simply leave the Irish banks and take your business to Europe. If you own a smartphone, you can go to https://n26.com/ and fill in a few short details, then follow the instructions, download the app and via your smartphone the bank at N26 (a legitimate internet-based bank which operates from Germany, one of many SEPA-area countries) will get in touch and talk you through everything in much the same way as a Skype call. This process takes about ten minutes from beginning to end and doesn't involve going to the bank, filling out a million forms, being quizzed twice about your own details and jumping through hoops. Karl did it and was so impressed that he is now a regular customer of theirs.

Obviously there are some downsides – you can't write cheques, and lodging a cheque can be tricky – but if you are willing to make the conversion to online banking you won't look back. Think of it in the same way as when you first began using a smartphone. One more thing: the user interface is so many light years ahead of Irish banks that you'll never understand your initial appetite for doing banking the way you used to. Another upside we should mention is that N26's banking is free.

THE SAVINGS EXPLAINED

It's easy to spend more than you expected (we won't count the money the bank make on your behalf from retailers when you use your cards). Adding up the ATM fees at the higher end equates to €1.05 a week or almost €55 a year. Then tag on some fees, like overdraft renewals, and factor in the cost of doing anything with a teller, processing a cheque or a myriad other things, and it could easily cost at least €2 a week (we think for many people it's almost double this). So our best estimate is that a very average person could save about €13 a month or roughly €160 a year. It's fast to fix, so do it soon.

Before you open a current account, start by comparing the costs of accounts. There may be certain costs on your account, including fees and charges, penalties and interest charged on overdrafts and loans.

Current account fees can include monthly or quarterly account maintenance charges; charges for each transaction such as a withdrawal, lodgement, direct debit or payment by debit card or cheque; service charges for carrying out instructions such as setting up standing orders, direct debits or issuing duplicate statements; overdraft fees, including a yearly facility fee; and the cost of replacing lost or stolen ATM or debit cards.

Another thing to look out for is penalties. Many banks charge penalties if you do not keep enough money in your account to meet your payments. You may have to pay for unpaid standing orders, unpaid direct debits and bounced cheques.

When you are shopping around, look at interest you are charged, such as on overdrafts.

 TIME *You need to allow at least a week for a current account switch. With N26 you'll have an account open in a matter of minutes, but there is the added work of moving all your bills across because they are not part of the switching code.*

 DIFFICULTY *The bank you are leaving and the one you are moving to will do most of the donkey work for you. This means that switching bank accounts is much easier than you might imagine.*

 SOME THINGS TO WATCH OUT FOR *It is worth checking what services you will get from your new bank. If a contactless debit card is important to you, make sure the bank you are moving to offers one. Check out too if you will receive a paper statement. Many banks want to issue statements electronically, but that may not suit you. Ask what interest rate is charged on overdrafts and related fees. A list should be provided.*

 USEFUL WEBSITES *Check out the websites of all the banks that offer current accounts – AIB, Bank of Ireland, Ulster Bank, Permanent TSB, EBS and KBC Bank. Then go to the financial product comparison section of the Competition and Consumer Protection Commission – www.consumerhelp.ie. And https://n26.com/.*

12

GENERIC DRUGS

TOPIC	Medical expenses
EXPECTED SAVINGS OR EARNINGS	€200
TIME REQUIRED	2 hours
LEVEL OF DIFFICULTY	● ○ ○ ○ ○

Medicines are expensive in this country. Despite the fact that Ireland has one of the biggest pharmaceutical industries in the world, we pay far more for medicines than countries like Spain or Portugal and even more than they pay on the other end of the island, in Northern Ireland. Yet few of us haggle. We emerge from the doctor's clinic ill and under pressure, and are not inclined to think about the price we are paying for a small number of pills. Maybe the pharmacy is near the GP's clinic, and you are feeling under the weather. But that convenient pharmacy might just be the most expensive place to have a prescription filled.

We need to think more about shopping around for medicines, availing of discounts that may be offered to people who work in the same company, or avail of the great value offered by discount pharmacies.

We owe your regular everyday chemist a 'thank you' for what has turned a customer question into a conversation about saving money. That's because now that a chemist is allowed to tell you if there is a generic equivalent it means you aren't swayed by popular names alone.

The drug industry is huge and highly regulated, and it's expensive to make drugs that people can use safely. It often costs over €1 billion to make a drug for some new cure marketable.

Costs like that have to be recouped, and because of this patents are given out to protect intellectual property. After a certain amount of time, though, those patents end and the same drug can be made by other firms. While the name won't be the brand name you are used to, chemically it will be identical.

WHERE THE PROBLEM LIES

Ireland offers poor value to people who have to pay for their own medicines. If you have a medical card, the cost of filling a prescription is covered by the State, save for a charge of €2.50 for each item that is dispensed to you, up to a maximum of €25 per month per person or family.

If you are not covered by a State scheme you end up paying full whack. And some argue that private patients subsidise the costs of State schemes such as the medical card and the Drugs Payment Scheme. And Ireland has an ageing population, which means higher spending on medicines.

On top of this, we like what we know, and part of what you know is influenced by advertising spend, which can be fairly pervasive. Some brands become so strong that their name becomes the meaning of the thing you are talking about. You clean the floor with a Hoover, but this isn't the machine, it's a brand name – a very strong brand name.

In the world of drugs it's the same. If you have a cold sore, allergies or even a cold or flu, there are certain over-the-counter brand name drugs that are synonymous with treating those conditions.

HOW TO FIX IT

There are alternatives to paying high prices for prescription drugs. Here are some options that will save you money.

If you are on a lot of medication, and do not qualify for a medical card, you should sign up for the Drugs Payment Scheme. This means that if you pay more than €144 a month on prescription medicines, the State takes care of the rest of the cost. That means that you will shell out €1,728 a year. But the good news is that you can claim 20% of this back off the taxman, or €345.60. Fill out Revenue's MED 1 form at the end of the year.

Back in 2013 new rules were brought in that mean pharmacists are obliged to dispense generic drugs where possible. Unless a GP has written the words 'do not substitute' on a prescription, you should be offered a cheaper, but identical substitute.

Karl found this out recently when asking for a well-known cold sore treatment for his son; there was a generic alternative he didn't know of and it was only one-third of the price of the one he used to buy.

This can mean it costs a fraction of the branded version of the medicine. And some generics are cheaper than others, so it is worth asking questions about exactly what you are being given.

However, many pharmacies stock only one generic alternative to the branded medicine.

Another option is to sign up for a discount pharmacy deal. These usually have an annual subscription charge of €25 and they offer you deeply discounted medicines, often delivered to your door. Some even offer to deliver to your home at no charge. Two of these are Healthwave and Limitless Health.

Healthwave's website (www.myprescription.ie) shows you if a generic exists and tells you how much it will cost. The business model of these operations is based on high sales volumes, which means big discounts for consumers.

Consumers should not forget to ask their GP if a cheaper generic option is available when the medical expert is writing out a prescription. Doctors are well aware of the cost pressures consumers are under at the moment.

People travelling abroad should get prescriptions filled in bulk in countries where medicines are cheaper.

While we are talking about chemists, it is also worth mentioning that you can go to a chemist and ask them for their opinion on a variety of things that might have you feeling under the weather. While they can't dispense drugs that need a prescription, they can often save you a trip to the doctor, which is another way they save you money.

THE SAVINGS EXPLAINED

Pharmaceutical companies exploit the fact that Ireland is a small market. This means the wholesale costs of medicines are high. This feeds into high prices in pharmacies for those paying for their own medicines and poor value for the State through the medical card, drugs payment and long-term illness schemes.

And the margins charged by retail pharmacists are also high, according to consultant clinical pharmacologist and expert on the price of medicines Professor Michael Barry of Trinity College Dublin. Professor Barry has stated that the margins being earned by pharmacists mean that private patients end up paying double the original cost of prescription drugs. He questioned dispensing fees of between €3 and €5 per item, and mark-ups of 50% of the cost of ingredients. What this means is that you can get better value employing some of the tactics just outlined. A family should easily save €200 over a year by being a smarter prescription purchaser.

Hardwire it into your mind to ask, 'Is there a generic equivalent?' It takes about three seconds to ask, so make sure to find out. Most chemists will be more than happy to tell you.

 TIME *No more than two hours should be spent signing up for a discount pharmacy retailer.*

 DIFFICULTY *It's as simple as asking a question: 'Is there a generic option or alternative?'*

 SOME THINGS TO WATCH OUT FOR *Doctors often write out prescriptions for small quantities of medicines. If you know you will be returning for more, ask for a repeat prescription, but be careful not to overuse the medication. Be aware that in some cases doctors are only allowed to prescribe enough medicine to last a certain amount of time.*

Buying from an online pharmacy is cheap, but it is fraught with danger, and not to be recommended.

 USEFUL WEBSITES *Consult the HSE's website, www.hse.ie, for information about generic drugs. Discount pharmacy Healthwave is at https://healthwave.ie. Pharmacies and pharmacists are regulated by the Pharmaceutical Society of Ireland. Its website, www.thepsi.ie, is worth checking out.*

The Health Products Regulatory Authority have a list of interchangeable medicines at www.hpra.ie/homepage/medicines/medicines-information/ generics-lists.

13

USE COLD WATER

TOPIC	Household spending
EXPECTED SAVINGS OR EARNINGS	€125 on laundry
TIME REQUIRED	1 hour
LEVEL OF DIFFICULTY	● ○ ○ ○ ○

In a typical home, laundry is one of the many near-continuous chores (ranked just below food preparation and cleaning), so how you do things makes a difference. Sadly, we haven't found a magical way to avoid laundry, but in this chapter we are making a suggestion about the way you use your washing machine.

WHERE THE PROBLEM LIES

Machines are set for what we are familiar with, for instance 90 degrees for cottons. People tend to use hot washes because they equate them with hot showers or baths and think that it takes a bit of heat to get something clean. This is a belief based partly in history because in the past we didn't have detergents that were as effective as the modern ones, and hot water really did play a certain role in the cleaning process, apart from killing off bacteria. Even today in some cases it makes better sense to use hot water, but it certainly isn't the case with many items of laundry that are only slightly soiled or not heavily worn (in playing sports or at the gym, etc.).

HOW TO FIX IT

It's simple. Use lower temperatures and look for detergents that work well at lower temperatures. You may not have noticed it before, but more and more detergents are saying on the label that they work at 20 or 30 degrees, which is really a way of signalling that they do the job at a lower temperature.

We are constantly reminded to be more energy-efficient. This is usually achieved by using less energy in a way that might not suit you (for instance, keeping your house colder rather than warmer), but with the right detergent a low temperature wash can obtain comparable results, so it's victimless. If you can obtain the same results for less money, it doesn't make any sense not to pocket the savings.

What makes this possible is that the hard-working scientists of the world have been busy figuring out how to give us whiter whites at lower temperatures. The chemicals used today for cleaning clothes operate differently from the old-fashioned ones; they are more efficient, more concentrated and generally doing a better job.

THE SAVINGS EXPLAINED

We are going to assume a 'per unit' tariff on electricity of about 17 cents per kilowatt hour (kwh). When a standard machine is used at a hot setting you could be using over 4.5kwh or about 77c per load. If you use cold water instead you can get the job done for more like 0.5kwh, which is nearer 8c.

EU ratings give you energy consumption figures based on a 2kg load washed at 40 degrees. Because many machines take a larger load than this you can't assume that just because your machine has an A+ or A++ rating it isn't costing you; the other common trend in washing machines is to take loads from 6kg to 12kg (on more modern machines).

We'll assume that the 69c difference applies if you are doing one load of laundry every three days. If you don't live alone this may be a higher figure; if you have several children, in particular young children, you may do nearer to one load of washing per day.

At the lower end the savings work out at about €70 for a two-person household. For an active family with kids it could make a difference of up to €250 per year. We'll figure that most households are somewhere in between those figures and go with savings of up to €125 a year.

 TIME *In terms of additional time it takes almost none, most of the 'time' described at the start of the chapter is to allow you the time to read this chapter and to pick up the right detergent the next time you go shopping.*

 DIFFICULTY *Changing the dial on your machine? This is one of the easiest wins for your wallet we can think of.*

 SOME THINGS TO WATCH OUT FOR *If you have a new machine or are thinking about getting one, ask some questions about how the power consumption is estimated because the rating for a 12kg load machine may still be based on the assumption that you only use 2kg per load.*

As well as this, get the staff at the shop to explain, or read the manual to figure out, how to do delayed settings. A lot of people have day and night rates for electricity, so putting machines on at the cheaper tariff if you have a night rate makes far more sense.

 USEFUL WEBSITES *Sustainable Energy Authority of Ireland, www.seai. ie. Use http://energyusecalculator.com/ to work out your sums for any appliance.*

14

SCRAP EXPENSIVE TV

TOPIC	Household spending
EXPECTED SAVINGS OR EARNINGS	€180 a year
TIME REQUIRED	1 hour
LEVEL OF DIFFICULTY	● ○ ○ ○ ○

According to Television Audience Measurement Ireland, the average person spends three hours and ten minutes a day watching TV. That's about 13% of the entire day, or, if we assume that you sleep about eight hours a day, 20% of your waking hours. Think about that, because it means if you are working an eight-hour day and commuting to and from work, much of the rest of your time is spent watching TV. Our national consumption of TV is therefore massive.

WHERE THE PROBLEM LIES

It's very common for households to have a TV subscription plan that isn't used fully or where there are add-on features that aren't being used. For instance, a lot of households have additional channels but they also subscribe to streaming sites, which might be offering similar fare.

Or they have a sports subscription, but the person who likes sports is not the same person who is 'in control of the TV', so it's basically a cost that is incurred and the benefit not received.

HOW TO FIX IT

There are obvious issues in being sedentary and sitting around watching TV. The single biggest fix would be to stop watching so much and spend your time doing something healthy, but we are discussing costs so we won't rattle on for too long about that. So what you do instead is look at your spending on TV. In terms of a 'cost per hour' it probably isn't that high because people watch so much of it, but when it comes to 'overall cost' it can be many hundreds a year, so decide if you really need it. If you do, this will be one of those chapters that won't help. Everybody has things they don't want to give up or won't give up, but the savings are substantial, so consider it.

THE SAVINGS EXPLAINED

A fairly standard cable TV subscription will cost about €25 a month. There are always promotions and give-aways and other things to make you sign up, but in the main, people who don't have expensive add-ons like sports coverage will spend at least €25; others will spend far more. So consider this. You could get a Chromecast for your TV and sign up to a service like Netflix, which is €9.99 a month. If you found what you like to watch on that and on the free channels, you'd be saving €15 a month every month. If you have kids there is also an endless variety of things they can watch, including documentaries and the like. It won't suit everybody, but if you try it you can tune into savings of €180. Or you could go a step further and choose to have no cable TV, in which case you could be ahead by €300.

Free TV

Many consumers have dramatically cut costs by ditching subscription TV services altogether to opt for free television services received via Saorview for Irish channels and Freeview for all the main British stations, including all the BBC and ITV stations. Premium paid channels such as Sky Sports or Sky Movies are not available, though the free packages do include many specialist stations such as children's channels RTÉ Junior and CBBC.

Although you can kiss goodbye to monthly bills with these services, they do involve one-off equipment and set-up costs starting from around €219 to €289 from installers such as Freetoair (http://freetoair. ie) or Billfree TV (www.billfreetv.ie).

TIME *It doesn't take long to make this change, but it may take a while to get used to it if you are a bit of a tele-addict!*

DIFFICULTY *This is very easy to figure out and implement; hence, we give it just one star.*

SOME THINGS TO WATCH OUT FOR *With some services, you can only use it in one place at a time. For instance, with Netflix you have to pay more to be able to use multiple streams at once, so if you have several users in one household working off one account then be aware of that. Also, make sure you aren't over-using your broadband as some plans still have very low usage allowances, in particular for the likes of satellite connections which in some rural areas are the only way to get broadband.*

USEFUL WEBSITES *www.netflix.com*

15

SAVE BY GOING ONLINE

TOPIC	Household spending
EXPECTED SAVINGS OR EARNINGS	€400
TIME REQUIRED	6 hours
LEVEL OF DIFFICULTY	● ● ● ○ ○

Many people do not use the web for managing and paying household bills. But this is a mistake as most companies reserve their best deals for customers who are prepared to make transactions online and switch from getting a bill in the post to online billing. It has been estimated

OK 1K 2K 3K 4K 5K 6K 7K 8K 9K 10K 11K 12K

that households that stay offline are losing up to €400 a year as those prepared to use the web get the better offers.

Older people, in particular, are reluctant to use the internet to conduct household finances. They are wary of being scammed or just making a mistake. Some people may regard the internet as a minefield, but it's also a mine of information and a rich depository of good-value deals.

People prepared to use the web to conduct business are the winners in the value stakes, with mobile phone companies, energy companies and banks all offering the best deals for online transactions.

The Consumers' Association of Ireland (CAI) has said that some companies are fleecing their customers by charging them for paper billing. Deputy Chairman of the CAI Michael Kilcoyne said that the public is being overcharged for some services. 'There are many service providers who actually use the opportunity to fleece their customers,' he said.

WHERE THE PROBLEM LIES

Banking, utility bills, TV and broadband bundles cost more if they are bought the traditional way. And it costs a lot to have bills posted to homes. Some companies charge up to €40 a year to send out paper bills every month. This means that companies are profiteering from people who don't have the skills, the broadband connection, or cannot afford to be online.

The high cost of signing up for goods and services without using online facilities particularly hits older people as fewer of them tend to go online to buy services and goods.

And lack of broadband in many rural areas means that almost one million people are in a situation of digital exclusion and these people are shut out from the best deals.

You could call the higher costs imposed on those who pay bills by posting cheques a postal premium. Add to this the government's stamp duty of 50c per cheque, which means that writing 40 cheques a year will cost you €20 in stamp duty alone, not to mention the cost of postage stamps. All this means that it is becoming more expensive to manage your affairs with a pen and paper.

HOW TO FIX IT

Companies offer discounts of up to 20% to those prepared to transact through a website rather than engaging with a company employee. This translates into savings of €100 a year on typical household bills like energy and car insurance.

THE SAVINGS EXPLAINED

Searching for the best deals online, accepting email billing and paying by direct debit is the best way to save you hundreds of euros.

Take banking. Going into a branch and making a transaction with the help of a cashier means you will incur a charge of 39c if you are an AIB customer. The same transaction conducted electronically costs 10c. Bank of Ireland, the other big beast in personal banking, charges 60c for in-branch cashier transactions, but 10c for internet transactions.

When it comes to car insurance season, if you don't look at renewing online you could be losing out. Insurance companies offer online discounts and cash incentives that could easily save you 10% on your premium. That's about €60 for a regular family car.

Most mobile phone operators offer discounts to customers who sign up online. Some operators offer 20% off some plans, which could save €120 a year.

Still getting a paper statement from your energy company? It could be costing you a fiver a month or €60 per year.

Some of the lowest-interest credit cards are those that require you to manage them and make payments online. AIB's Click card has an interest rate of 13.6% for purchases, almost half of the interest charged for purchases by some card issuers. But you will not automatically receive a paper statement every month.

Some customers of TV services are paying more than €40 a year to get their bills in the post.

 TIME *It will take a while to shift from paper billing and managing your household finances online, but it is worth it for the savings. Expect to spend at least a few hours researching deals and signing up for them online.*

DIFFICULTY *It is not difficult to switch to electronic options for conducting your family's business. Comparison sites like Bonkers.ie and Switcher.ie are your friends in this endeavour.*

 SOME THINGS TO WATCH OUT FOR *It might be savvy to get the best deals by doing business online, but do make sure that you regularly check your bills. Getting an emailed invoice sometimes means we are less inclined to check out the details we are being billed for, but it is vital to do this. Do make sure you use only trusted websites and be wary about ever giving away the likes of bank account PIN (personal identification number) codes online. Never respond to emails seeking banking details. Telephone the supplier first if you are suspicious about what you are being asked to provide online.*

 USEFUL WEBSITES *The websites of suppliers are the best place to start, while price comparison sites are well worth a visit.*

16

MOTOR INSURANCE

TOPIC	Transport
EXPECTED SAVINGS OR EARNINGS	€500
TIME REQUIRED	5 hours
LEVEL OF DIFFICULTY	● ● ● ○ ○

Motor insurance premiums have shot up massively in the past three years. Annual increases of close to 40% have been recorded in official figures. Insurers have reacted to the collapse of Quinn Insurance, Setanta, Enterprise and the precarious funding position of RSA and FBD by heaping price pressure onto the nation's more than two million drivers. Average premiums are now close to €900, according to market research company

Consumer Intelligence. And Dublin motorists are paying even more.

Even for drivers with a clean licence, no penalty points and no claims, hikes of €300 in premiums have become commonplace. Some drivers are being hit with higher rises, especially if they have had a claim on their policy, are a young driver, or have penalty points.

There have even been claims that the average cost of premiums could hit €1,000. AIG, the world's biggest insurer, said that Ireland should consider banning some claims to avoid the average cost of premiums hitting €1,000.

WHERE THE PROBLEM LIES

There is a complex range of reasons for these premiums increases.

These include loss-making in the insurance sector due to under-pricing in the past, as companies cut prices to the point where they could not make money. They did this to try to win market share. The industry is also suffering from investment losses being made by insurers. In the past insurers could deal with losses on their insurance books by making them up by investing and making a return on premium income. Low interest rates means that this is no longer possible.

Insurers have also failed to put sufficient funds into their reserves to meet rising levels of claims. Rising values and more frequent claims are a real problem, while fraudulent and exaggerated claims are an ongoing issue in the Irish market.

New regulatory rules and changes to the courts system have also hit insurers.

In effect, insurance companies are effectively asking drivers to bail them out for their poor management decisions and losses.

However, the good news is that there are a large number of motor insurers active in the market, while credit unions are now involved in reselling motor cover at good rates for members.

Not all insurers are making losses at the moment. Aviva is managing to buck the trend.

All this means that shopping around for car cover is more important than ever.

HOW TO FIX IT

Here are some ways to fight back against the savage premium rate rises and save money.

Switch

If you are claims-free, it makes sense to regularly switch insurer. Compare rates from different insurance companies by ringing them or going online. It is worthwhile using a broker. It won't cost you any more than going directly to the insurer as the broker is paid by the company. You may be entitled to a discount if you have more than one type of insurance policy with the same company.

Also ask if there are other discounts you might be able to get.

Don't over insure

Other tips to keep the costs down include being conservative with the car's value. This is important as you can only claim what the vehicle is deemed to be worth by the insurance company's assessor.

People often overvalue their car. Check car sales adverts to get a good market indicator of your motor's value. Alternatively, the Revenue Commissioners website (www.revenue.ie) has a valuation tool for each model and year of manufacture, put in place for vehicle registration tax purposes.

Check the excess

Be careful about the excess. This is the amount you have to pay before you can make a claim. Lately, insurers are imposing higher and higher excesses. This reduces the risks for them, but means you end up not claiming for small accidents. Excesses of €500 are not uncommon, but when they get to that level, they rather negate the value of having insurance.

Get a discount by using telematics

Telematics is a way of monitoring the location, movements, status and behaviour of a vehicle. You can do it with a smartphone. Insurer AIG offers discounts of up to 20% on motor cover for using an app that monitors driving style. AIG says it aims to reward better driving behaviour with potential savings of up to 25% on car insurance premiums. Customers who use the app will be given a 20% discount on their premium immediately and further discounts of up to 5% will be applied to the premium after three months' use, subject to the scores achieved.

Someone who drives smoothly and anticipates traffic flows should achieve a good score.

AIG says XLNTdriver is the first driving app on the market with an auto start/stop functionality, which means that users do not have to stop and start the app each time they wish to make a journey.

Men

Get insured with Its4women. Online insurer Its4women markets its motor insurance at women, but the law means it cannot refuse to cover men. Because most of its customers are women, who are safer drivers and have fewer claims, it tends to be more competitive than motor cover sold equally to both sexes.

A recent European Union gender directive, which became law in this country, means that men and women can't be discriminated against in terms of the price of insurance. Dublin student Shane Spain was able to reduce the cost of his cover from €810 to €500 by opting for Its4women.

Take out two-year cover

To ensure that you pay the same this year as next, you could opt for two-year cover, which is offered on motor insurance by Blue Insurance. This means that the premium you pay this year will be the same again next year. And if you have an accident in the two-year period, your premium will not rise. The motor insurance product is underwritten by UK business Zenith Insurance.

Don't modify

Avoid modifying your car, unless you are increasing its safety. Even a small modification to your car, such as new alloys, can cause your premiums to shoot up. Any changes should be discussed with your insurer first. However, any modification that increases safety, such as installing an alarm or immobiliser, can help you cut costs.

Small engine

Choose your car wisely. The more expensive your car and the bigger its engine, the more you are likely to pay. You may also have to pay more if your car is imported or if there are more theft claims on your model of car. Check with your insurer before you buy a car, so you can estimate insurance costs.

Pay annually

Pay for your cover annually if you can afford to do this. Paying for cover monthly is the same as taking a high-interest loan from your provider, with interest as high as 20% imposed on top of the premium for paying by instalments.

The savings explained

If you have an accident, and no one else is involved, it makes sense to consider paying the cost of the repairs yourself. This way you will avoid losing your no-claims discount, which may entitle you to a discount of between 50% and 75%, depending on the insurer. If you lose your no-claims discount you will have to rebuild it from scratch, something that could be more costly than paying for the repairs.

Also worth noting is that having more than one policy, like a home insurance policy, with the same insurance company will likely get you a discount. This means you may need to make your insurer aware of what policies you have, as they make not be aware that you have more than one policy.

Liberty and AXA offer discounts of 10% off the cost of insuring second cars, or if you also take out home insurance. Aviva gives a 25% discount on premiums for second cars.

Young drivers can cut the cost of premiums by between 25% and 30% by passing their driving test. Completing an insurer's driving course can mean further discounts. Young drivers can also cut the cost of cover by adding their parents to their cover.

 TIME *You should allow five hours for contacting at least a dozen insurers to get quotes at least two weeks before you are due to renew. Ring insurers, go online and use insurers' online services, and also contact a broker.*

DIFFICULTY *Seeking out better-value motor insurance is not difficult, but it is time-consuming. Once you have your driver details and car facts to hand, you should be able to obtain a range of quotes easily.*

 SOME THINGS TO WATCH OUT FOR *The job categories that insurers use to price your cover can be broad and many motorists could save money by describing their occupation differently. For example, describing yourself as a housewife or a househusband instead of being unemployed can help reduce your premium. It's worth experimenting to see if a different job title affects your premium, but you should never lie about your job. Don't say you're a butcher if you're a baker. This is considered fraud and you could be prosecuted.*

 USEFUL WEBSITES *The website of the Competition and Consumer Protection Commission, www.consumerhelp.ie, has a useful section on motor insurance. It also publishes a survey of insurance costs every so often.*

17

HOME INSURANCE

TOPIC	Property
EXPECTED SAVINGS OR EARNINGS	€160
TIME REQUIRED	4 hours
LEVEL OF DIFFICULTY	● ● ○ ○ ○

The cost of home insurance has been going up over the last year or so. The increases are nothing like those for motor cover, but the cost is rising nonetheless.

House and contents insurance is something we all need to have in place. Renters simply need to take out a contents policy, as the landlord normally shoulders the responsibility for insuring the building.

But homeowners and the owners of residential investment properties need a policy that covers the contents and the building.

However, there is much confusion among householders about how much cover is necessary.

Another issue is that consumers are likely to be overpaying for their home insurance if they get it through a bank. Multiple surveys have shown that banks are among the most expensive providers of home insurance. The results of the surveys show that householders may be overpaying by up to €300 a year by opting to take cover out through their bank. This is because there are price gaps of up to 100% across the market, according to Jonathan Hehir of brokerage Insuremyhouse.ie, who carried out one of the surveys. Home buyers are often persuaded to take out home insurance with their lender when they are signing up to a mortgage. If you are doing this, just make sure you are getting good value.

When you are insured with the bank where you got your mortgage, the tendency to move is not huge. There is a comfort there for some people. What this means is that getting too cosy with your bank could be costly.

Savings of €160 are easily attainable by switching to another provider. And switching home insurance is a doddle, yet only 16% of us, or about one in six households, move provider each year.

WHERE THE PROBLEM LIES

Many people stay with the same insurer, accept the renewal notice they get and simply pay the higher premium each year. This is a percentage game for insurers; they know a certain percentage of people will accept the higher premium and pay up, despite the insurer being engaged in a try-on when sending out renewal notices.

Householders are also prone to mistake the market value of their property for the reinstatement figure, which is the figure used for insurance purposes. Yet there is no relationship whatsoever between the figures.

The market value is the price the property is expected to achieve when placed on the open market and will be determined by market forces. The reinstatement figure is the cost that would be incurred to rebuild a home subject to current building regulations.

The Society of Chartered Surveyors Ireland (SCSI) produces a guide of recommended reinstatement costs (www.scsi.ie). These figures vary depending on the type of building insured and its location, according to Philip Farrell of the society.

HOW TO FIX IT

Your best bet is to switch. There are no brownie points for loyalty when it comes to home insurance. In fact the opposite is the case. Your insurer is more likely to hike the cost of your cover each year than reward you for staying with them.

Insurance companies are hitting householders and motorists at the moment because they have had a lot of additional claims. This means you may get a higher renewal quote than expected, even though you have not had a claim, and this is a great opportunity to move insurer.

Get your current home insurance documents and use them to check how much you are covered for rebuilding costs, contents cover and any other features, such as all-risks cover. All-risks cover is an optional extra on your contents insurance, to cover certain items for loss, damage or theft, when they are outside the home.

Go to the SCSI website and use the online 'Rebuilding Costs Calculator' to see how much you should be insuring your buildings cover for. Look at the Competition and Consumer Protection Commission's home insurance cost comparisons, which you can find on its website at www.consumerhelp.ie, to give you an idea of how much you should be paying. Then visit a number of insurance websites – either brokers or insurers – and obtain some online quotes.

If you get a better quote, call your existing insurer and see if they can match it or even beat it. The insurer may want to retain your business if you haven't had a claim. If you live in an area damaged by flooding, you may have this excluded from your policy. However, another insurer may see it differently, so never accept the first 'no'.

THE SAVINGS EXPLAINED

When it comes to moving provider, the most important thing is to understand the policy you have. Ask yourself if it is doing what you want it to do and be sure it represents value for money.

Ask the following questions:

- What is the excess? This is the first amount you pay of any claim. The higher the excess, the lower the premium, but offset that against the risk you are taking.
- Is there an 'old for new' clause? In other words, if your old lawnmower is stolen, can you get a new one to replace it, or will they simply give you a discounted value?
- Does your insurer apply the 'average clause' in the case of under-insurance? This means that if the contents of a property are worth €30,000 but they are insured for just €15,000, then you will be underinsured by half.

You may be asked if you want an optional extra called all-risks cover. This is an add-on on most home policies and protects you against loss, theft or accidental damage to valuables such as jewellery. The key aspect of all-risks cover is that it covers you for both inside and outside the house. It will usually cover items taken abroad for up to 60 days, according to the Competition and Consumer Protection Commission. You are likely to have to pay extra for all-risks cover, depending on your insurer. If you make a claim, your insurer may choose to either give you the cash value of the item or pay to repair or replace it.

You can choose an overall value for 'unspecified items' without having to list each one. If you have items worth more than your insurer's single-item limit, you should think about listing the items you want covered and their value.

 TIME *It should take no more than 30 minutes to move to a provider that gives you better value when renewal time comes, or to trawl though the market, get a better quote, and then get your existing provider to match it.*

 DIFFICULTY *Changing insurance provider, and/or negotiating with your existing insurer is easy. It just takes a little bit of effort.*

SOME THINGS TO WATCH OUT FOR *Reviewing your cover regularly is important. Insurance products include cover for the cost of rebuilding a house in the event of damage or a fire and also of replacing your contents.*

These costs can change from year to year. If the costs of rebuilding have gone up, you will need to increase the amount of buildings cover accordingly – otherwise you could face a shortfall if you need to make a claim after a fire, for example.

Ways to cut your policy include having another insurance policy with the same company, fitting secure locks on doors and windows, installing an alarm and fitting smoke detectors.

 USEFUL WEBSITES *The Society of Chartered Surveyors Ireland keeps an up-to-date rebuilding costs calculator and consumer guide on www.scsi. ie. The website of the Competition and Consumer Protection Commission (www.consumerhelp.ie) has a cost comparison survey. The commission is a State body charged with protecting consumers, which means that its price comparisons and the information it provides are unbiased. It's also worth checking the websites of major insurers, and those of brokers.*

18

DITCH THE COFFEE AND THE TAKEAWAYS

TOPIC	Lifestyle
EXPECTED SAVINGS OR EARNINGS	€1,000
TIME REQUIRED	A little a day
LEVEL OF DIFFICULTY	● ○ ○ ○ ○

This tip is often overplayed. It's one that both Charlie and Karl don't like (we're both coffee addicts), but because it is true we have to include it at some point in the book. It's about the little things, things like takeaway coffee.

If you don't drink coffee this tip won't help. If you do and you regularly buy it from shops, then think about this: a coffee made at home and taken in a Thermos (I know it lacks the frothy milk, etc.) will cost about 40c; one made at work in a filter or with instant is in most cases virtually free. A premium coffee, on the other hand, will cost around €3 (unless you're near a McDonald's or somewhere that does discounted hot drinks).

Another area of savings is food eaten away from home. Karl's workplace has a gas barbecue in the back yard – he can eat roasted courgette, asparagus, sweet potatoes and chicken at a total cost of about €3.50 (vegetables don't cost that much unless you buy premium and organic ones). Many people in the same office spend €5 on a sandwich for lunch. Another guy spends €10 on a carvery lunch. The point is so simple and so clear that it doesn't make sense not to mention it.

WHERE THE PROBLEM LIES

Convenience is so … convenient. It takes time to prepare food. If you have a busy life, whether with kids, work, studies or extracurricular activities, this means giving up precious time in order to buy, prepare and make meals.

For just a little bit more money you can get somebody else to do it all for you; it's one of the lovely things about a modern economy – there's a lot of convenience. But because we are trying to squeeze every penny of savings and extra income there is available it means having to give up a habit that isn't necessarily good for you.

Something like a hot chicken roll may seem at first like a decent meal, but you are taking in a lot of calories, empty carbs and high fats in sauces. They might taste lovely – but that's the downside of everything that isn't good for you.

The second issue here is what eating like this does to you. It's no surprise that the availability of convenience foods, along with more sedentary lives, has risen in tandem with obesity in both children and adults. Exercise alone doesn't counteract unhealthy food – you can't out-train a bad diet – so think of that when making your choices.

HOW TO FIX IT

Be prepared. For breakfast you could make 'overnight oats' and throw in some Greek yoghurt and fruit. It's a delicious way to start the day, so good that it probably seems like cheating. There are also lots of things like 'fake-away' recipes – fake takeaways – foods that taste bold but are actually healthy.

There is a massive cost to obesity which isn't well calculated in Ireland, but in the UK estimates are that it costs over £8 billion a year. Being too heavy is seen by some (see the links at the end of this chapter) as being as bad for you as smoking, so remember these things when you transition to a healthier and cheaper choice; you are winning on several fronts at once.

THE SAVINGS EXPLAINED

First take a look at coffee. If you strip out holiday time, weekends and bank holidays, there are about 225 working days a year. If you drank one takeaway coffee every working day, you'd be looking at about €675 a year versus €90 for home-brew. So you could save €585 a year – a big difference for the sake of a cup of Joe. Karl said he may choose to ignore this one (good coffee is the only vice he has left).

Now to food choices, if you pack your own lunch or cook an inexpensive one at work – or at home if you're working from home or aren't working – you'll save at least €2 a day. Over the roughly 225 working days in a year, this comes out at about €450.

Add these two amounts together and you get €1,035 of savings in the year. We have rounded that down to €1,000 because not even the most dedicated frugal saver will go a whole year without buying something like a coffee or a lunch, so we factored some 'normality' into the sum.

 TIME *While it does take time to make a coffee yourself, it usually takes less than the time it takes to go somewhere and buy one. So the time on this one is minimal at best.*

 DIFFICULTY *Giving up nice takeaway coffee may be easy or difficult depending on how caffeine dependent you are. In reality, this is easy – like many things, it's just about changing a habit.*

SOME THINGS TO WATCH OUT FOR *If you get a takeaway coffee, you are limited to what's in the cup. If you make a pot of it you can always go heavier on the coffee, which isn't always a good thing. One of your authors can testify that overdoing the coffee in order to get a cheaper one can lead to some sleepless nights.*

 USEFUL WEBSITES *Search for 'fake-aways' or check out some of the recipes on www.netmums.com. Then chat to your boss about making sure your workplace has an area where you can eat or keep food. And a coffee percolator can be bought for under €40.*

19

OVERPAY YOUR MORTGAGE

TOPIC	Property
EXPECTED SAVINGS OR EARNINGS	€550 (but €11,000 over the life of a loan)
TIME REQUIRED	2 hours
LEVEL OF DIFFICULTY	● ● ● ○ ○

Overpaying your mortgage to clear it faster can make a lot of sense, particularly as interest being paid on deposits is so pitifully low at the moment. There is a great psychological boost to be had from clearing a mortgage, so the earlier you get it paid off, the better you may feel. Many people took out 30-year and 35-year mortgage during the housing boom, leaving them likely to be still required to make monthly repayments in retirement. Making monthly overpayments is one way to ensure you have paid off the home loan before you end up leaving the workforce for good. However, before you embark on mortgage overpayments be aware that you will not get the money back if you need it for something else. That amounts to a loss of liquidity.

WHERE THE PROBLEM LIES

If you are lucky enough to have spare funds you are unlikely to generate much in the way of a return from keeping a lump sum in the bank. Anyone earning interest of 1% a year will be doing well. Then there is deposit interest retention tax (DIRT), which further eats into any return you get. And if you have spare money each month after paying your outgoings, the temptation to spend it is strong.

Another problem Irish households have is that we are still heavily indebted, a legacy of the boom and bust. Households in this country recently fell from being the third most indebted in the European Union to the fourth. Debt as a proportion of household income is at 149.4%. This means that a household that earns income of €50,000 after tax and after social welfare payments will still owe €75,000.

Another problem we have is that our mortgage terms are too long. In 2005, four out of every five first-time buyers took terms lasting 30 or 35 years. Before then, the traditional term of a mortgage was 25 years.

Another issue is high variable mortgage rates – something that affects around 300,000 people in Ireland. One way to get the mortgage rate down is to shrink your loan to value (LTV) – the amount of debt you have in proportion to the value of your home. Banks now offer lower variable rates for those with lower LTVs. They call these LTV-variable rates.

Overpaying your mortgage offers a potential solution to over-indebtedness, long mortgage terms and high variable rates.

HOW TO FIX IT

If you have spare cash, and you are on a high variable mortgage rate, it makes sense to contact your mortgage lender and put in place arrangements to pay off a lump sum off the mortgage, or up your monthly repayments.

This makes particular sense if your mortgage interest rate is higher than the return you get from your savings in a bank or credit union, after paying DIRT.

It's worth noting that if you are overpaying every month you can stop paying at any time. Tell your bank you want the overpaid money to come off the principal outstanding, and not to be paid in interest only. Do not rely on the bank knowing what you want.

THE SAVINGS EXPLAINED

In very simple terms, overpaying your mortgage is the same as shortening the term. In other words, if you have 17 years left on the home loan, you can get it down to 15 years by overpaying for a while.

You can reduce your mortgage by making a lump sum payment off the debt. This is called reducing the capital. Make sure you tell your mortgage lender that you want the lump sum to be paid off the capital, also called the principal. By paying a lump sum you can either lower your monthly repayments or shorten the term so that your mortgage is paid off sooner. Either way, you will pay less interest over the term of the mortgage than before. Another alternative is to pay a larger amount than the agreed repayment each month.

By doing this, you will pay your mortgage off faster and save money on interest. For example, if you have 20 years left on a €200,000 mortgage with an interest rate of 4%, by paying an extra €100 each month, you would save over €11,000 in interest and reduce your mortgage term by over two years, according to the Competition and Consumer Protection Commission.

In the past people on fixed rates were not able to overpay their mortgages. However, that approach is changing. Both Bank of Ireland and KBC Bank allow you to overpay fixed-rate mortgages, provided you keep to certain limits. A limit of 10% of the usual monthly repayment is not unusual.

Although the savings are impressive over the life of the loan, we are going to break the amount down into the amount you would save each year. To get a feel for the average amount being saved we just divide €11,000 by 20 years, which is €550.

TIME *Arranging to make regular overpayments, or paying a lump sum off your mortgage, is not likely to take more than an hour or two.*

 DIFFICULTY *This task is not at all difficult.*

 SOME THINGS TO WATCH OUT FOR *Pumping extra cash into a mortgage means you lose access to those funds. And remember it is important to have enough money to hand to cover at least six months of expenses. Life has a habit of throwing up surprises and unexpected expenses, so having the wherewithal to handle these is important. Also, if you have a tracker mortgage you are likely to be paying so little in interest that you might not be wise to overpay your mortgage. Investing in State savings, or in a low-cost passive investment fund, may make more sense.*

 USEFUL WEBSITES *The Competition and Consumer Protection Commission has a useful tool it calls an extra mortgage payments calculator on its website, www.consumerhelp.ie. This works out the impact of a rate change or a change of term on your mortgage – you just have to enter a few relevant figures on your home loan.*

20

SAVE FOR
A DEPOSIT

TOPIC	Property
EXPECTED SAVINGS OR EARNINGS	€10,000 a year
TIME REQUIRED	2–4 years
LEVEL OF DIFFICULTY	● ● ● ● ●

Savers are having a tough time of it. Interest rates are at rock-bottom levels, with some corporate customers having to pay banks to hold their cash. Add to that the fact that the exchequer extracts high taxes on any interest returns paid on savings and you have a situation where saving almost seems like a mug's game. But anyone who wants to be approved for a mortgage needs a big deposit before the lender will be able to sanction the loan. Deposit requirements of €40,000 are not unusual, even if that is a very big ask.

WHERE THE PROBLEM LIES

Blame the property crash and belated attempts by the Central Bank, the regulator of our banks, to ensure that our banks do not collapse again by over-lending on property assets for high deposit requirements. The bar has been set very high. First-time buyers can borrow 90% of a property's value. Everybody else has to have a deposit of at least 20%.

Take a property that is €300,000 to buy. A first-time buyer will need a deposit of 10%, which is €30,000.

It is worth noting that banks do have some flexibility, which allows them to exceed the limits, but they are unlikely to do this for a first-time buyer looking to get more than 90%. They are more likely to look favourably on people trading up or a former owner who wants more than 80%. The banks get to choose who qualifies for an exemption, and they are quite hard to get.

HOW TO FIX IT

Saving is not easy. It takes commitment and some homework, especially as the interest being paid by banks is so low. Here are some suggestions from a financial economist at the Rennes School of Business, France, Professor Michael Dowling:

1 Put money into a savings account that is not linked to your current account.

2 Set up automated savings transfers for each month, with money going from your current account to your dedicated savings account.

3 Try a social savings approach – tell friends what you want to have saved for in the next year. Studies show this to be surprisingly effective. This is one of the main principles behind the success of weight-loss programs such as WeightWatchers.

4 Think about a 'save-more-tomorrow' type of arrangement. This is where you set aside a portion of your next pay rise to go to increased savings.

5 Finally, you might look into a hard commitment and see if the 'no pain, no gain' approach would work for you.

THE SAVINGS EXPLAINED

It is important to know how different savings accounts work to ensure you get the best return.

A *demand account* has a variable rate of interest and allows you to withdraw your money immediately if you need it. A *notice account* has a variable interest rate, but you must give notice if you want to withdraw money. In return, you get a better rate of interest. With a *fixed-term deposit account* you get a fixed rate of interest if you leave your money for a set period of time, say one or two years. If you need to withdraw your money earlier, you will usually get less interest.

Here are more tips to get into the swing of saving.

Budget
It is important that you keep your finances in good shape. The best way to do this is to record all spending and all income. Yes, it's boring, but you would be surprised how effective writing down what you spend can be when it comes to helping you cut out extraneous expenditure. You can find budgeting tools on the website of the Money Advice and Budgeting Service – www.mabs.ie.

Lifestyle
Totting up your spending on a regular basis shows you how much you spend on the little things – the expenditure that really adds up. Turn off lights at home, go out for meals less often, shop sensibly, use your credit card less often, and you will reap the rewards. It may seem like a period of self-imposed austerity, but anything worth doing takes sacrifice.

Transport
If you drive a car, consider switching to public transport or even using a bike, if they are options. Buy a Taxsaver commuter ticket through work for further savings on your buses, trains and the Luas.

DIRT free
There is a government scheme that gives you back the tax you pay on deposit interest (deposit interest retention tax) if you are saving for a deposit for a home. What it means is that people who buy a home can claim a refund on the tax the government usually takes from the interest earned on the savings they used to provide a deposit. The scheme is

open to any first-time buyers who purchase a house or apartment to live in as their home and people who self-build a home to live in. The relief applies to savings used by first-time buyers towards the deposit on a house bought or built between October 2014 and December 2017.

 TIME *According to the Central Bank it will take most people about two to four years to save for a deposit for a house. That is a long time, but you end up with an asset and if you get the mortgage paid off before you retire, you should have no housing costs later in life.*

 DIFFICULTY *This is probably the most difficult task in this book, but the rewards are immense.*

 SOME THINGS TO WATCH OUT FOR *If you fall off the savings wagon, don't give up and don't despair. Just start again. Nobody is perfect. Accept that there are going to be ups and downs, and don't beat yourself up if you fall behind target.*

 USEFUL WEBSITES *There are savings calculators on the website of the Competition and Consumer Protection Commission, at www.consumerhelp.ie. A good budget calculator can be found at www.mabs.ie.*

21

GET MORTGAGE-READY

TOPIC/SUBJECT	Property
EXPECTED SAVINGS OR EARNINGS	€000s
TIME REQUIRED	Weeks
LEVEL OF DIFFICULTY	● ● ● ● ●

Saving for a deposit is only one aspect of getting mortgage-ready. When you have cleared that hurdle there are others to negotiate. These include ensuring you have a clean credit record, having key documents in place, demonstrating good financial management and choosing the appropriate mortgage. Demonstrating to your lender that you can tick all these boxes is the only way you can be sure you will qualify for a mortgage. Property prices are rising, which makes it important that you get organised now so you are in a position to buy before prices escalate beyond what you can afford. Getting the mortgage you need to buy your home is your first step.

WHERE THE PROBLEM LIES

Before you start to look for a home to buy you need to ensure you can borrow the money to fund it, unless you are lucky enough to be very rich or have extremely wealthy parents. Check with potential lenders to get a statement of how much they are prepared to lend you. This is called approval in principle and it will give you a good indication of what price range you can consider when looking for somewhere to buy.

It's worth noting that approval in principle does not mean that the lender has approved a mortgage and agreed to lend you this amount. The official mortgage approval is contained in a letter of offer, which the lender will only issue when it is fully satisfied with certain matters, including a valuation of the property you are buying.

HOW TO FIX IT

To get to the position where you have mortgage approval in principle you need to meet certain standards set by your lender and their regulator, the Central Bank. Here are some pointers.

Demonstrate you can afford the repayments

The most important thing to consider is how comfortable you are with the proposed repayments. Rates will change during the mortgage term. You will need to clearly demonstrate to the lender that you can afford your mortgage payments even if interest rates increase by 2%.

Is your income secure?

You need to be in secure employment. Being on a permanent contract is a requirement with most lenders. However, some lenders will consider contractors where there is evidence of contractual work for over one year on a continuous basis and where prospects for further continuous contract work into the future are strong.

Clean up your current account

Make sure your current account looks good. Avoid missed payments, referral charges and ensure there is no evidence of betting activity. If you think your credit history is not perfect, check it on the website of the Irish Credit Bureau, www.icb.ie. This will cost you €6. If there are missed payments or incorrect information, get it changed, or explained, immediately. If you are overdrawn, clear the overdraft and stay in credit.

Documents

The key documents are bank accounts, pay slips, your P60 and a salary certificate from your employer. You will also need proof of address from a utility bill.

Gambling

Get rid of any apps on your phone (and anything on your bank statement) that indicate gambling, either the Lotto or with bookies. Some lenders interpret this as indicating that your finances are unstable.

Other loans

If you have personal loans or credit card debts, consider paying them off, even if it uses up some of your deposit. Not all lenders require this, but they do like to see disposable income intact. A broker will advise on what to do.

Income

When assessing multiples of income for lending purposes, err on the cautious side. Income from rent, shares, bonuses or overtime are not normally allowed. Be prepared to get your employer involved in proving where your money comes from and how much it is. This may involve P60s, payslips or other letters of comfort (assurances).

Accounts

If you work seasonally or are freelance or self-employed, expect your personal finances to come under more scrutiny. Engage an accountant to do up proper accounts which can be offered to the lender.

Be careful about online approval

Be aware of the extensive documentation required for lenders before mortgage approval is granted. You can largely ignore 'online approval' as it can all change when the information becomes due and is simply a bank gimmick to get you browsing.

Meeting conditions

Approval in principle varies from bank to bank, but it typically lasts between three and six months. After this there will be a number of conditions which need to be met before drawdown of funds, typically life assurance/assignment being put in place, house insurance, surveyor's reports and confirmation of legal title, along with signed contracts.

Pay off expensive loans

There is no point saving money furiously if you are paying ten times more in interest to service a long-running credit card debt. Neither will outstanding loans and a credit card deep in the red do any favours to your mortgage application. If you're indebted with expensive loans, try to pay them off as soon as you can – that's the advice of lender EBS.

THE SAVINGS EXPLAINED

Do make sure to get the cheapest mortgage you can. Do a comprehensive survey of the market and choose the one which gives you the cheapest interest rate over the lifetime of your mortgage. That means you may have to reject a financial 'sweetener', like an offer of a percentage of the overall mortgage to be drawn down in cash returned to you. Other incentives that need to be weighed up against the mortgage interest rate include funds towards the conveyancing costs and half price offers on home insurance. Otherwise, you could pay more for your mortgage over the term just to get some cash upfront. With some banks you get a discount on the mortgage interest rate if you have a current account, and mandate your salary to be paid into it, with the lender.

You will be repaying your mortgage for most of your working life, so secure the cheapest mortgage you can and choose a lender with a track record of treating its borrowers well.

TIME *Getting mortgage-ready will take a while, probably a number of weeks, even months.*

 DIFFICULTY *The process of getting approved for a mortgage is not easy. After all, buying a home is the largest financial transaction most of us will ever undertake.*

 SOME THINGS TO WATCH OUT FOR *Line up your insurance early. You will need to put mortgage protection insurance and home insurance in place before you can draw down a mortgage. Mortgage protection insurance repays your loan should you or your partner (if it is a joint mortgage) die before it is paid off. Home insurance covers the cost of rebuilding your home if it is destroyed by the likes of a fire. Some people leave getting insurance in place until they are about to draw down the mortgage. This is a mistake. If you run into difficulty getting mortgage protection insurance or home insurance, it is very likely that the mortgage will not be able to be drawn down, and that the house purchase will fall through. And you will probably not get the best value by opting for the home cover and mortgage protection insurance from the bank where you are getting your mortgage. Have your mortgage protection insurance and home insurance in place a few days before the house purchase closes. Your lender will not allow you to draw down your mortgage until you provide it with evidence that you have bought the insurance.*

 USEFUL WEBSITES *There are lots of places to find out how to get mortgage-ready, including the websites of mortgage lenders and larger brokers. There is also a wealth of information on www.independent.ie, the Independent News & Media site. This includes news stories and features on mortgages, property prices and lending rules.*

22

CAR FINANCE

TOPIC/SUBJECT	Transport
EXPECTED SAVINGS OR EARNINGS	€3,000
TIME REQUIRED	1 week
LEVEL OF DIFFICULTY	● ● ● ○ ○

There are lots of options when it comes to financing the purchase of a car, whether it is a new motor or a second-hand one. Lately, there has been a surge in car buyers using PCPs (personal contract plans) to finance their new motors. But motorists using PCPs may end up out of pocket when the time comes to trade in their car.

Financial experts have advised that anyone buying a new or second-hand car should not forget that there are plenty of other options they should consider before rushing to sign up for a PCP deal.

WHERE THE PROBLEM LIES

PCPs are essentially a modern twist on the old hire purchase agreement. You pay a deposit, which is typically between 10% and 30% of the value of the new car. You then make monthly payments, usually for three years. At the outset you agree the number of kilometres you are going to clock up over the period of the agreement. If you keep to this, the car will have a pre-agreed value at the end of the deal, known as the minimum guaranteed value, sometimes called the guaranteed minimum future value (GMFV). At the end of the three years you have a number of choices. You can buy the car outright for the guaranteed value agreed at the start. Alternatively, you can hand back the keys and walk away.

The option that most people take, and the one the dealer will be hoping you opt for, is to exchange the car for a new model. You finance this with a new PCP deal.

The key is that the agreed minimum value at the end of the term of the deal is sufficient to cover the final payment. And crucially there would be enough value in the car to include an amount of 'equity' which can act as a deposit on the next vehicle. This assumes you roll over your agreement into a new one, which most customers are expected to do.

However, if the value of the car falls below the amount agreed at the start of the deal, the equity will disappear. You could end up with no deposit at all for your next car. Fine, you can walk away from the deal, but you will have nothing out of the PCP to put towards your next car. Motor experts have warned that there is likely to be a glut of three-year-old cars in the next while as PCP deals taken out recently mature.

This is likely to push values down, meaning that many cars bought with PCPs will be below their guaranteed minimum future value.

HOW TO FIX IT

The key thing to remember about a PCP is that you do not own the car unless you buy it outright at the end of the agreed term.

The small print – the bits to remember and watch out for – include the following:

• High mileage could mean a lower minimum guaranteed value.
• A lot of wear and tear may also mean you do not get the full value of the car agreed at the start of the deal.

- If you have a crash and the cost of the repairs is greater than 66% of the original list price, you may also not get the minimum value you were hoping for.
- Because a lot of the repayments are deferred, the interest costs may be low initially, but the total ends up being high over the full length of the agreement.
- Dealers and car company banks are able to offer lower interest rates on the deals for the first three to five years because they retain ownership of the vehicle, lowering their risk.

Here are some alternative options.

Credit unions

Credit unions were traditionally where people went to for car finance. And they have plenty of money available, as most of them are under-lent.

Their rates are competitive, despite each one setting its own loan rates. Car loan rates are often lower than other rates in the credit union, with some charging as little as 5%.

The big advantage with funding through a credit union is that you own the vehicle, rather than leasing it, or effectively renting it, as you do through a PCP deal.

To borrow from a credit union you need to become a member first and save with it.

To join your local credit union, you must be living in the area that it serves, but you might be employed in a company that has a staff credit union or a member of a professional body that runs its own credit union. The process is much like applying for a loan with a bank in that you'll need, in this case, three recent bank statements and three payslips.

Then it will discuss suitable loan amounts and durations before processing your application. It will also ask permission to check your credit history with the Irish Credit Bureau.

You will also need to provide evidence, such as a sales invoice, that you bought the car. This is to stop people pretending to borrow to buy a car, but then using the money for something else.

Hire purchase

Car buyers don't always realise that the car finance they are offered in a car salesroom is actually a hire purchase agreement. This was traditionally a forecourt favourite.

The key difference between a hire purchase (HP) agreement and a personal loan is that when you buy a car with a personal loan you own the car as soon as you hand over your money.

With an HP agreement, you do not own the car until you pay off every last cent on the HP deal. At the end of the agreement, the finance company passes ownership of the car to you, provided you have made all the repayments.

Interest rates on HP deals are attractively low. Car manufacturers charge interest rates of as low as 0% APR (annual percentage rate) on some models. This is very competitive compared with the interest charged for a personal loan by a bank.

But with HP it is worth remembering that you can have the car repossessed if you continually miss repayments, while there are a range of fees and charges built into the deals. If you are having difficulties meeting the agreed monthly repayments you may be charged a fee of €60 if the lender agrees to change the terms of the agreement, according to the Competition and Consumer Protection Commission. You can have a penalty fee imposed for missed monthly repayments. In addition to this, an interest surcharge might be added in.

You don't have to rely on the dealer for a HP deals. Banks and finance houses are now offering them. AIB has a fixed interest rate of 8.45% on its hire purchase deals, with a typical agreement for more than four years.

First Citizen, which also offers deals through the State's 1,100 post offices, is offering hire purchase deals with typical interest rates of 8.5%. A minimum deposit of 20% is required.

Personal loans

Banks are trying to tempt us to take out car loans again. Take a loan for €10,000 to be paid back over three years. Banks typically offer an interest rate of 9%, with monthly repayments of €316. The total cost of the credit works out at €1,309.

THE SAVINGS EXPLAINED

Car retailers have come up with ingenious and tempting ways to get us to buy their products. Free insurance, low-priced PCP deals and generous car scrappage deals are just some of the temptations they put before us to get us to buy the latest reg car. But ask yourself if you really need a new car. Remember that the value of a new car depreciates rapidly. Also, watch out for the shortcomings of PCPs. The key thing to remember is that you will probably be locked into renewing the deal every three to five years for the rest of your driving career. And the popularity of PCPs means there could be a glut of cars on the market when you need to enter a new three-year PCP term.

 TIME *Buying a car is a big move. Allow yourself weeks of research. People often make the mistake of spending ages finding out about the car, and little time looking at the finance options. This leaves them vulnerable to be persuaded to take the finance package offered on the forecourt.*

 DIFFICULTY *Working out the best way to finance a car purchase is a difficult task. It is one that requires preparation and research, but once you get on top of it you can be confident that you are not being ripped off by a fast-talking car salesperson.*

 SOME THINGS TO WATCH OUT FOR *If you are buying a used car it is important to check that there is no finance owned on it. If there is, you could end up paying for it and still having it taken off you. Use a website such as www.cartell.ie car check to find out its history.*

 USEFUL WEBSITES *You will find good information about car buying at www.citizensinformation.ie, www.consumerhelp.ie and the website of the Society of the Irish Motor Industry (SIMI), at www.simi.ie.*

23

CHRISTMAS SPENDING

TOPIC/SUBJECT	Household spending
EXPECTED SAVINGS OR EARNINGS	€300
TIME REQUIRED	2 hours
LEVEL OF DIFFICULTY	● ● ○ ○ ○

Christmas is a key expenditure event that most of us face. If you have a significant other or children (and even when you don't), Christmas often results in higher than average outgoings.

The last thing we want to say is 'Don't spend any money at Christmas' because we know that isn't possible. What we do want to say is that some simple preparation can really help to ensure you have all the fun available on the budget you can afford.

That is the key point – maximising what you can afford and not going beyond it – because many of the financial problems in any new year start in the previous one.

Retail Ireland once produced the statistic that as a nation we'd spend over €4 billion over Christmas – that's about €1,000 for every man, woman and child in the country. Most of the population aged under 15 aren't earning a living for themselves, so obviously this means that the figure is concentrated among the remaining adults, which means that it's a higher sum for those doing the actual spending.

WHERE THE PROBLEM LIES

There are a few forces at play. A very large one that doesn't usually get a mention is the ability to say 'no'; this means saying 'no' to things that will cause you financial strain. So if you are being asked to go on yet another night out, having had a few already, perhaps it would do no harm to say no. If a friend's flown in from abroad and you won't see them for a long time, by all means say 'yes', but remember to say 'no' to another event that doesn't mean as much to you.

Spending at Christmas isn't just on presents; we tend to have higher outgoings on entertainment and all manner of things, including taxi fares and money spent in pubs and restaurants. Thinking through what you want to do in advance will help you prioritise how to spend not only your time but also your hard-earned cash.

HOW TO FIX IT

Here are six simple ideas you can use.

1 Ideally use savings or income to do your spending. If it's too late to do that this year, then start a savings account and put in a little something every week or month during the coming year. Sometimes it's too late to play catch-up, but you can always do it better the next time.

2 In the UK it's estimated that about 50% of people use credit around Christmas time. If you are using a credit card and can pay it off you don't have to worry so much, but if you know you won't be able to pay it off, don't use it. Instead get a cheaper term loan from a credit union or bank: their rates are about 11% whereas cards are usually over 20% – almost double the rate.

3 Santa isn't the only one with a list. Making a list at home helps to do a few things, including focusing your mind on what you need to get done as opposed to just browsing, which can result in overspending and gifts that aren't as well thought out.

4 Make a general budget – and don't forget to add in the other costs like food, entertainment and the like. The figure we mentioned at the start showed that the national spend isn't just on presents or on food, it's a mix, so budget for that.

5 Shopping online always gets a mention. Karl still likes going to real shops at Christmas – he does online shopping during the year (and am a convert to online grocery shopping) – but knowing the price of things online is a good way to do a bit of groundwork research. If you see a price that is way out of kilter with the online price then you know it's not a great deal. Equally, if you see one that's better you're probably getting a good deal. In shops you can also haggle, something you can't do online, and, of course, remember to factor in delivery costs for online shopping!

6 Kris Kindle is a good way of doing things if you are from a big family or have groups of friends who traditionally buy each other gifts. Apart from setting a limit on cost, it also means you usually get one nice thing rather than five sets of socks or some other forgettable gift. We know it's the thought that counts, but in our book the pressie does too!

Something that rarely gets a mention is buying for yourself. Some research indicates that almost one-fifth of presents bought are for the person buying them. It's hard to avoid being generous to yourself, so either set aside some money for that purpose or do your best to resist. Better yet, if you have the discipline, put that money aside and blow it in the post-Christmas sales, when you'll get far more for your money.

If you are in a serious cash crunch you could also give 'post-dated' gifts. For instance, if there's a particular child, whether a niece or nephew or one of your own, you want to treat to a special time, you could give them a card telling them that you'll spend a day together at the zoo or at some other event, even a hike or some other adventure. If you can't think of anything straight away, call it a 'mystery tour'.

For adults with children you could give them babysitting vouchers or if you have a trade or skill that you know they could use you could offer to do some work for them. The limit is your imagination. The real idea of presents (traditionally) is that they're a token to show you care for a person, and nothing says 'I care' more than showing up to do a job that a loved one needs.

Older people who might already 'have everything' often enjoy events more than items. For them in particular some kind of trip or going to a play or local event is more touching and memorable than another scarf.

THE SAVINGS EXPLAINED

If you manage your budget carefully it should be realistic to shave at least 20% off the expected spending. Assuming this is over €1,000 per adult we get to the figure of about €200. Then, if you do some targeted present-buying, don't buy for yourself and take the time to do some research on prices and haggling, you should be able to get your savings up by another €100. These combined give us the €300 figure. If you do this as a couple or family it will be higher.

TIME *The two hours estimated will be spent doing a bit of research and setting things up, such as the Kris Kindle draw.*

DIFFICULTY *This can be as easy or hard as you make it – if you are organised it will be handy, if not you'll struggle. That's why we didn't give it just a single star, as much of the result is up to you.*

THINGS TO WATCH OUT FOR *You'll still need to shop around and look for deals. One thing that is always a risk is not allowing enough time – get that wrong and the whole plan can fall apart.*

USEFUL WEBSITES *For Secret Santa or Kris Kindle the website www. drawnames.com does it all for you. For events, sites like www.dublinevent-guide.com or the various 'What's On' websites are good. You can also find local city/town/village sites in your own area that list events; and your county council will also have event guides on their websites. For savvy shopping, the likes of Amazon and eBay are always a good starting point, and if you work it cleverly you can usually find the bargains and have a lot of purchases done early. If you want to buy from the UK but the company doesn't deliver to Ireland, remember that there are services like Parcel Motel (www.parcelmotel.com) you can use.*

24

START
A PENSION

TOPIC/SUBJECT	Tax breaks
EXPECTED SAVINGS OR EARNINGS	€600 a year
TIME REQUIRED	8 hours
LEVEL OF DIFFICULTY	● ● ● ● ●

How long will you end up working before you get to retire? The answer to that question could be a very long time. Few of us outside the public sector have pensions. And the State retirement age – when you receive the State contributory pension – has risen to 68. Many people will end up working into their 70s if they do not put a private pension plan in place.

Sure, the State pension will be enough, you might tell yourself. But it is designed only to be sufficient to keep you out of poverty. Could you live on €238 a week now? Even without a mortgage and other debt that you may hope to have cleared by the time you retire, €238 will not get you very far. And it is likely that more and more people will still be renting at retirement age.

WHERE THE PROBLEM LIES

Many people avoid thinking about pensions for much of their working lives. A survey commissioned by the Irish Association of Pension Funds, a body that represents pension savers, found that millennials were least concerned with retirement planning. The other issue is that the later you leave it to start saving into a pension, the more expensive it becomes. Every ten years you delay starting a pension leads to a doubling in the cost of building up a retirement pot.

Other strong reasons for not saving for retirement include the cost of living for those in their 30s and 40s, with competing financial priorities leaving little to spare for saving for the future. Also playing a role in stopping us setting up a fund is inertia, and a perception that pension providers offer poor value for money due to high charges and poor investment returns. The government keeps promising to set up a scheme into which the one million or so workers with no private pension provision will be automatically enrolled, but the deadline for this keeps getting moved.

Many people don't understand pensions. The blame here lies with previous generations who have created a complex set of legislative and taxation rules that would baffle some of the smartest brains, according to Jerry Moriarty of the Irish Association of Pension Funds.

HOW TO FIX IT

If your employer offers you membership of a pension scheme, you would be wise to accept. Taking up such an offer will mean three entities contributing to your future financial wellbeing – you, your employer and the Revenue Commissioners in the form of income tax relief. Most independent advisers recommend – and government policy statements concur – that an adequate income in retirement is around half of what you were earning before you gave up work.

That may be a tall order for many of us. It means that if you earn €33,700 at retirement, you will need to top up the annual State pension amount by €4,500 a year. This is to end up with a total retirement income of €16,800 a year. To achieve that you will need to budget for a fund of at least €120,000.

That sounds like a lot. But if you start from the age of 25 to put aside €100 a month, and your employer matches this, you should make it, according to calculations from the Pensions Authority.

THE SAVINGS EXPLAINED

If your employer has a pension scheme, it usually pays to join it. Failing to join is like turning down extra pay. And often, the employer will increase how much it pays in if you increase what you pay in.

You also get tax relief at your marginal rate of tax. What this means is that if you are on the higher tax bracket and you pay €100 into your pension, it will only cost you €60, with the other €40 being provided by the government. In many workplaces, employers match their employees' pension contributions, so if that were to happen in this instance, €200 would be invested into your pension, but would only cost you €60.

Any investment returns are also free of tax. At retirement you can take some of your savings as tax-free cash and the rest is taxed as income. Once you have been in a scheme for two years, you can take the value of your and your employer's contributions with you if you change employer.

 TIME *Starting a pension is not something you should rush into. You need to give it some time; a day at the very least. And the more research you do, the better you will be prepared for the pension challenge.*

 DIFFICULTY *Pensions are fiendishly complicated, which means that it is worth your while getting good professional advice. An adviser who comes with a recommendation from friends and colleagues will help guide you through the pensions maze. Do get the best pension advice you can as starting a retirement fund is one of the most important financial decisions you will make.*

SOME THINGS TO WATCH OUT FOR *Charges vary hugely, and can have a significant impact on how your pension fund performs. There are charges for setting up a pension, charges imposed on each contribution, and annual management charges imposed on the fund value. All this means that people paying into a pension should consider the effect of charges. Some companies cover the cost of the charges for staff pension fund members. A report commissioned by the Department of Social Protection concluded that charges range from 0.9% to 3.08% across the types of pensions examined. The impact of charges at those levels on your final fund is between 5% and 28%. However, it is worth noting that some providers with high charges actually deliver better returns.*

 USEFUL WEBSITES *The website of the regulator for pensions, the Pensions Authority (www.pensionsauthority.ie), has good information on the ins and outs of pensions. For specific queries, posts on www.askabout-money.com, which is populated by people with good knowledge of financial affairs, is a good place to visit.*

25

CREDIT
CARDS

TOPIC/SUBJECT	Banking
EXPECTED SAVINGS OR EARNINGS	€900
TIME REQUIRED	2 hours
LEVEL OF DIFFICULTY	● ● ● ○ ○

Credit cards are expensive. In fact, a credit card is a hellishly expensive tool. Only moneylenders charge more interest, and they are only turned to by people who are desperate. But despite the cost, for many of us credit cards have become an indispensable tool for living. This is especially the case for online shopping, which is taking a stronger hold on our buying activity by the day. Used sensibly, a credit card is well worth having. This is especially the case if you are disciplined enough to pay down your balance regularly, by going into your online bank account and transferring funds from your current account, or setting up a direct debit to make payments when they fall due each month,

WHERE THE PROBLEM LIES

The convenience of a credit card can lull us into repeatedly spending more than we can afford to on the card. The danger is that we then repay less than is owned. This can lead to the card debt getting out of control. Interest charged on credit cards is high because it is unsecured lending, with a high risk for providers of consumers defaulting on the debts.

Card providers play on our weaknesses by setting out 'minimum payment' amounts with each balance statement. This is always set at a low and manageable figure. But it is nearly impossible to get on top of the card debt if you only pay the minimum. Paying the minimum means you will end up paying more in interest and it will take ages to reduce what you owe on your card. If you owe €1,000 on a card with an interest of 17%, it will take two years to clear it if you repay just €50 a month.

The other major problem with credit cards is that they come with a range of other fees and charges, apart from the high interest rate imposed when you make purchases with your card. These include late payment fees, a charge for going over your credit limit and foreign exchange fees.

HOW TO FIX IT

One option for those with stubborn card debt is to switch to another card provider. These will entice you with low, or even zero interest rate deals for a period. The idea is that you transfer the balance you owe on your existing credit card to a new one. You must have an unblemished credit history for them to take you on. It's also worth noting that you are likely to be hit with a high interest rate on purchases once the introductory offer comes to an end.

Another option is to ditch your credit card. Stop using it and pay off what you owe by taking out a credit union loan. A good alternative is a debit card, which has much of the functionality of a credit card. With a debit card, you can only spend on it if you have funds in the bank. If you spend more than you have in your current account, you will incur expensive overdraft fees, if you have an overdraft facility in place. Visa debit cards also offer chargeback, where you can have a disputed or fraudulent transaction reversed. Consider also a prepaid credit card, such as Payzone Money or 3Money. These are useful online, but the fee for loading them up is often high.

THE SAVINGS EXPLAINED

Switching credit card provider and transferring the balance owed on your card account to another card issuer charging low, or zero, interest for a period can reap big savings. Suppose you owe €5,000. It could take you almost two years at an interest of 22.8% to clear that balance if you pay €300 a month. Switching to a card with a 0% or low interest balance transfer offer could save on the interest you are currently paying. If you are disciplined, you could save €900 in interest. The key is to pay off the balance within the low, or no, interest period, and not make new purchases on the new card.

Check out card interest rates and credit limits on www.consumerhelp.ie or www.bonkers.ie. Assess how long the low rate will apply. Ask yourself if you will you be able to pay back what you owe before the rate increases.

Check whether the reduced rate applies only to the transferred balance or also to new purchases and cash withdrawals during the offer period. A key question is what rate will apply after the introductory offer ends.

 TIME *The process of applying for a new card, filling out an application form, complete with proof of address and income documents, should not take long. Researching the best card option is the time-consuming bit. But the whole process should not take much longer than two hours.*

 DIFFICULTY *Avoiding getting crushed by high interest on an expensive credit card is not easy, but you may be surprised that is it not as difficult as you may have feared.*

 SOME THINGS TO WATCH OUT FOR *Don't use your credit card to take out cash. The interest charged on credit card cash withdrawals can be as high as 21%. Note that most credit card providers (with the exception of AIB and Permanent TSB) hit you with interest as soon as you use your credit card to withdraw cash – even if you repay your bill on time.*

Credit card cash withdrawals are treated differently from purchases. When you use your credit card to buy something, you can avoid getting charged interest as long as you repay your bill on time (usually within 56 days). On the other hand, if you use a Bank of Ireland, KBC, Avant Card, Tesco or Ulster Bank credit card to withdraw cash, you have no grace period. You are charged interest from the time you take out the cash. With AIB and Permanent TSB, you can avoid getting hit for interest on credit card cash withdrawals if you repay your bill within 56 days of taking out the money. The exceptions are AIB's Budget Mastercard and Low interest Mastercard as neither has an interest-free period for cash withdrawals.

If you are switching credit card, make sure you close your old credit card account so that you are not tempted to spend money using both cards. Remember that you have to pay stamp duty before you close your old credit card account. Ask your old credit card issuer for a Letter of Closure, which proves that you paid the stamp duty for that year. Give this letter to your new credit card issuer as soon as possible so they do not charge you stamp duty again.

 USEFUL WEBSITES The website of the Competition and Consumer Protection Commission, www.consumerhelp.ie, has lots of information on credit cards, including a card comparison section. Price comparison site www.bonkers.ie also has a credit card comparison tool.

26
HELP-TO-BUY SCHEME

TOPIC/SUBJECT	Property
EXPECTED SAVINGS OR EARNINGS	Up to €20,000 (we'll say it's more like €10,000)
TIME REQUIRED	12 hours
LEVEL OF DIFFICULTY	● ● ● ● ○

The government brought in a 'help-to-buy' scheme this year with the aim of helping first-time buyers (who are usually the younger home buyers) to purchase a home by making the deposit easier to obtain. While formally launched in 2017 it is backdated to 19 July 2016, so anybody who bought a new home or self-built a home since then can apply.

The scheme offers a rebate of up to 5% of the purchase price or contract price (whichever is the lower) from income tax and DIRT tax paid in the past four tax years to a maximum of €20,000. The property must cost less than €500,000, or €600,000 for retrospective applications. The size of the loan versus the value of the property must be 70% or more.

So, for every €100,000 of value you must be borrowing at least €70,000, the idea being that very cash-rich buyers don't need this help.

WHERE THE PROBLEM LIES

Ireland has had housing problems for as long as we can discern from record keeping. One of the most recent issues has been rising prices and rising rents. People who may want to buy a home are finding that they can't save for a deposit, and even those who are happy to rent experience rising rents, like a 'tax' on the type of housing tenure they choose. This leads to lower lifetime savings; not owning a home can exclude a person from one of the strongest wealth-creating processes in many economies. The reason for this is that when you make a mortgage payment it's like a 'forced savings'. You pay off some of the capital and this improves your personal equity (or savings) in the property. Even if prices never rose again, or if they stayed flat or fell, if you make enough payments, one day you'll owe nothing and in turn will have a valuable capital asset. That's why, when comparing renting to owning, it makes sense to compare only the interest portion of a mortgage (which, like rent money is consumed and you have no claim to it) against the rent, because the other part, the 'payment' has a savings or investment effect on your personal balance sheet.

HOW TO FIX IT

The government wanted some kind of scheme that would increase the number of new homes. In economics it would be described as 'shifting the supply curve'. Typically, when more producers enter a market there's more supply, and when you offer tax benefits on something you also get more supply. The issue is that when you have general housing shortages in areas of high demand, a scheme like this may not 'fix' things. That said, our job is to help you get the money if it's available; we'll leave the state of the nation's finances up to the Department of Finance.

There are two main stages, and they only apply to a property built by a 'Qualifying Contractor'. 'Qualifying Contractor' is a designation obtained from Revenue by the contractor. The contractor applies for this desig-nation and must be tax compliant and submit information to Revenue for 'qualifying residences', which are the properties that this scheme can be used for.

The first stage is the application stage. You must register on 'MyAccount' if you are a PAYE worker or Revenue Online Service for the self-employed. You then fill in Form 11 or Form 12 (Revenue forms) for the tax years that apply. Hopefully you are up to date because any outstanding taxes have to be paid before you can use the scheme.

You then go through the application stage, give your property purchase and bank details, and information that helps to determine the refund. After that you'll find out what amount of refund you may be due, and using that information you go and sign a contract for the home and get a mortgage approval. After this you move on to the 'claim'.

The second part is the 'claim' stage. Having given all the information, you confirm that it is all still correct (it includes things like purchase price/property/mortgage amount and your PPS number). This is verified by the developer, or solicitor for a self-build. Ultimately payment is made directly to the qualifying contractor for the rebate amount and you complete the purchase. Voilà!

THE SAVINGS EXPLAINED

As mentioned above, you can get up to €20,000, based on the purchase price. Some people have said that if this pushes up prices it won't help a first-time buyer, but let's do the maths first. Let's say that a house that costs €200,000 now goes up to €210,000 because of it. The first-time buyer qualifying for the full 5% will get a €10,500 refund.

They'll need to put down a further €10,500 instead of the €21,000 they would have had to put down before, so in that respect they are still better off. Their mortgage loan is slightly higher but they will have less time in the rental market and trying to save, as well as lower taxed income that has to be put aside to create a deposit. In short, if you can obtain this scheme you'd be mad not to take it up.

Remember that to be a 'first-time buyer' you (and your partner, if you have one) must never have bought or owned a home before in any country. So if you bought in Canada in the past and came home having never bought here, you are not a first-time buyer in the eyes of the Irish tax authority. You must also occupy the property yourself for at least five years – it cannot be a rental home.

WHEN DOES IT START?

It started on 19 July 2016 and runs until 31 December 2019, and it is open for applications now. Three groups are covered. First are the retrospective applicants – people who either signed contracts for a new home after 19 July 2016 or (for self-build) drew the first part of their loan after 19 July 2016. The new applicants are the further two sections that apply: the first-time buyer who is buying a new build; and the first-time buyer who is a self-builder.

 TIME *This is not going to be a quick fix by any means, and it will only apply to first-time home buyers, and within that group only to those who are buying a new home or self-building a new home. So be ready to spend time on this one if it applies to you. It's hard to say how long it will take, but in terms of total time spent working on it, about 12 hours would be a fair assumption from beginning to end.*

 DIFFICULTY *The main difficulty is qualifying because it doesn't apply to every home buyer. If you do qualify it will be complex if you aren't used to doing paperwork, but Revenue are helpful and you can always call them to help guide you through it. We're still going to give it four out of five stars, though, due to the time and paperwork required.*

 SOME THINGS TO WATCH OUT FOR *Make sure that you get everything right, that your taxes are paid, that you (or both of you if you are one person in a couple) are a first-time buyer. Make sure your contractor gets on the list if they aren't on it already. After that it's just a case of getting through the bureaucracy of it.*

 USEFUL WEBSITES *The main site you'll be checking into for this will be www.revenue.ie, where the help-to-buy scheme is managed and run from. They also have all the notes, terms and conditions listed on it.*

27
MEDICAL TREATMENT ABROAD

TOPIC/SUBJECT	Medical expenses
EXPECTED SAVINGS OR EARNINGS	€1,000, at a minimum
TIME REQUIRED	5 hours
LEVEL OF DIFFICULTY	● ● ● ● ●

Thousands of people are on waiting lists for operations in this country. The ongoing scandal of ever-lengthening waiting lists is despite expenditure on health services in this country being the second highest in the OECD (Organisation for Economic Cooperation and Development), which has 34 members, mainly developed countries. An overburdened hospital system means that even those with chronic complaints may have to suffer on until they reach the top of the queue. But it is possible to have your treatment carried out in another EU country, and have the cost of the procedure reimbursed by the HSE in Ireland.

WHERE THE PROBLEM LIES

People in the public system have to wait, whether they have a medical card or not. Long waiting lists for taxpayer-funded treatments in public hospitals have been a feature of the health system in this country for decades, and the problem shows no sign of going away.

Fewer people now have health insurance, a legacy of the financial bust that began in 2008. Some 270,000 people ditched their cover between 2008 and 2014, the worst years of the crisis. The number of people with health cover has begun to climb again. However, even those with health insurance may find that a procedure they need to have carried out is not fully covered by their insurer. Vast numbers of people downgraded their level of cover during the economic blow-out, and now find that certain treatments do not form part of their health insurance package, especially in the areas of orthopaedics and some ophthalmic procedures. Others have taken out low-priced insurance, with reduced public hospital coverage or no cover in a private hospital – they can have the cost of the procedure covered in a public hospital as a private patient, but they are likely to end up in a public ward and could still be subject to public hospital waiting lists, depending on the hospital. Many others who had to ditch their cover and have now re-joined are serving lengthy waiting periods before they qualify for their insurer to pay for pre-existing conditions. Paying for an operation in a private hospital is expensive. A hip operation will set you back €12,000.

HOW TO FIX IT

If you are on a waiting list, with no likely date when your treatment will be carried out, and have no health cover, you have two options. You can self-pay, or have the cost of the procedure carried out elsewhere in the EU and get refunded by the HSE.

Self-pay

Close to 10% of the medical operations and diagnostic tests carried out in the 19-member Independent Hospitals Association of Ireland are paid for by the patient, according to the association's chief executive, Simon Nugent. This is often in the form of a whip-round among family members to pay for a mother's hip operation, or a loan from a credit union.

A number of credit unions have loans tailored to cover the cost of private hospital procedures. In Galway, the St Anthony's and Claddagh lender has a special interest rate of 6.5% for members who need a health loan. Lucan Credit Union in Dublin has teamed up with the Hermitage Clinic to fund members who need work done in the clinic. And Waterford Credit Union has partnered with the Whitfield Clinic in the city to fund operations. Check your credit union to see if it has a special loan for a health procedure.

Treatment abroad scheme

People who are on a public hospital waiting list in this country are eligible to get treatment anywhere in the EU and be reimbursed by the HSE.

Known as the Cross-Border Healthcare Directive (CBD) scheme, it covers dental care, physiotherapy and mental health services, as well as operations, according to the HSE and the Citizens Information Board. Patients are eligible to receive any treatment abroad that they would be eligible for within the Irish system. This means that the scheme provides an opportunity to avail of services in Northern Ireland. Those wishing to take part do not have to be on a waiting list or processed through an outpatient department.

Patients are reimbursed to the amount that it would have cost the State if the care had been carried out in an Irish public hospital. But as this is an expensive country to have treatment carried out, that is not usually an issue.

THE SAVINGS EXPLAINED

To take part in the scheme, patients must be referred by their doctor (a GP or a consultant). Depending on the treatment needed, individuals may be required to give copies of their medical records to foreign healthcare services. You choose the specialist to treat you, possibly in conjunction with your Irish GP or consultant who is referring you on.

You are not excluded if you have health insurance, but you must access the scheme as a public patient only. This means you must be referred on by a medical practitioner through the public system. Only public consultant appointments can be accepted, the HSE says. However, you can be referred by your GP, but you can't pay a consultant here to refer you to one abroad.

Virtually all elective treatments are covered, with the exception of organ transplants. The scheme covers psychiatric and addiction treatment, as well as orthodontic treatment and rehabilitation.

This scheme differs from the European Health Insurance Card scheme, which covers you if you fall ill suddenly in another EU state. And note that the separate Treatment Abroad Scheme is for treatments not available in Ireland.

Your travel and accommodation costs will not be reimbursed. You must pay for the procedure upfront and then seek a refund from the HSE.

TIME *Working through all this will take time; it is not something that should be rushed. If you are considering using the cross-border scheme there is much to consider. You need to consult medical specialists here, and the HSE. You also need to research the qualifications of the medical staff in the other country.*

DIFFICULTY *Using the cross-border scheme is not easy. There are a series of steps and a number of criteria: see the extensive 'frequently asked questions' list on the HSE website. Approval is not granted when one or more of these steps hasn't been followed, or one or more of these criteria have not been met.*

SOME THINGS TO WATCH OUT FOR *Inpatient healthcare under the Cross-Border Directive does not require prior approval. But an option has been put in place for patients to receive prior authorisation to ensure that they have full knowledge of the costs involved in their treatment, and of the reimbursement rate applicable in advance of undertaking such treatment. You are advised to contact the HSE's National Contact Point, Cross-Border Healthcare Directive Department, which is based in Kilkenny (tel: 056 778 4546; email: crossborderdirective@hse.ie).*

USEFUL WEBSITES *Details about the Cross-Border Healthcare Directive scheme are on the HSE's website at:*
http://www.hse.ie/eng/services/list/1/schemes/cbd/faqs/.
There is also information on the Citizens Information Board website at:
http://www.citizensinformation.ie/en/social_welfare/social_welfare_payments/disability_and_illness/treatment_benefit_scheme.html.

28

PUBLIC TRANSPORT COSTS

TOPIC/SUBJECT	Transport
EXPECTED SAVINGS OR EARNINGS	€300
TIME REQUIRED	One hour
LEVEL OF DIFFICULTY	● ● ● ○ ○

Public transport is expensive and patchy in Ireland. Rural areas are often poorly served by buses and trains, while low State subsidies mean that commuters are hit with price rises at the beginning of each year. However, there are some options to defray some of the cost.

OK   1K   2K   3K   4K   5K   6K   7K   8K   9K   10K   11K   12K

WHERE THE PROBLEM LIES

As a small island with a dispersed population, transport costs are always going to be high in Ireland. We have too few cities and large towns, and too many people living in one-off houses to make public transport a viable option for many. No wonder we are so attached to our cars. There are buses, trains and trams in Dublin, but they are not cheap. The annual cost of a bus, rail or Luas ticket in the capital city is more than €2,000. In Berlin, the equivalent ticket costs less than €1,000, according to the lobby group Rail Users Ireland. The blame for this is put at the door of successive governments, as State subsidies are low here compared with other advanced economies. Commuters get hit every year with some of the largest price hikes. They are seen as a captive market, as they have no choice but to pay the increases. There is a regulator, the National Transport Authority, but it struggles to keep prices down as public transport providers continually rack up losses.

HOW TO FIX IT

Unless you qualify for free public transport there are not many options for making savings. But two excellent ways to cut the cost of bus and rail journeys are to use Leap cards and to avail of the Taxsaver scheme. Leap card fares are generally around 20% less than standard cash tickets.

Taxsaver

The Taxsaver Commuter Ticket Scheme is the name of the State incentive that gives tax relief for the purchase of monthly/annual transport tickets. It incentivises people to use public transport to and from work by allowing them to buy tickets with employees' wages before income tax, pay related social insurance (PRSI) and the universal social charge are deducted. And your employer saves on the 10.75% employer PRSI charge when purchasing the ticket.

It applies to public transport commuter tickets if you are travelling for work by public transport bus, rail or Luas. But it is not confined to State-provided public transport services. It can include private operators if they are approved transport providers.

Your employer registers for Taxsaver on www.taxsaver.ie and buys tickets for you. The cost is deducted directly from your salary, and you get to save between 29% and 52% on the regular price, depending on ticket type and your tax band, according to the Taxsaver website.

Taxsaver is operated by Dublin Bus, Bus Éireann and Iarnród Éireann (Irish Rail) and approved transport providers in conjunction with the Revenue Commissioners.

Leap card

A Leap card is essentially an electronic ticket. It applies to public transport services in Dublin, Cork, Galway, Limerick, Waterford and Wexford. There are adult Leap cards, but also versions for students and children (ages four to 15).

As well as being cheaper than single tickets paid for in cash, Leap cards have what is called a capping system built into them that limits the value used from your ticket. If you make lots of trips with your Leap card on a daily or weekly (from Monday to Sunday) basis on DART/Commuter Rail journeys, a maximum cap value will be applied to your travel credit spend, according to Iarnród Éireann. The system automatically caps your spending, ensuring that you don't spend any more than you need to.

Additionally, when you use the card to pay for two or more journeys within 90 minutes of each other on Dublin Bus, Luas or DART/Commuter Rail, an automatic discount will apply to the second and subsequent fares.

A Leap card is useful as Dublin Bus requires exact fares. If you don't have the exact fare you get a refund-due receipt that you have to redeem at Dublin Bus headquarters on O'Connell Street in Dublin. Leap card covers other Dublin Bus services, including Airlink, Xpresso and Nitelink.

You can buy a Leap card at 650 outlets in the cities where the scheme applies. You can top it up in the same outlets, online or at a transport station. There is also an auto top-up feature you can put in place. With this, your Leap card will automatically top up with funds from your bank account whenever your credit balance falls below €10. You can choose to auto top-up by €30, €40 or €50.

THE SAVINGS EXPLAINED

Leap card and Taxsaver are sure ways to save money. And you can combine the two, as some commuter tickets are now issued in the form of a Leap card.

TIME *If your employer offers the Taxsaver scheme, it will not take long to sort out. Contact your human resources function. A Leap card can be bought online or in a shop, something that can be done quickly. Registering it also takes only a short while.*

 DIFFICULTY *The Taxsaver scheme has its downsides. The income tax relief is granted at your marginal income tax rate. This means those on the lower 20% rate lose out. So if you are buying a ticket that has a gross cost of €2,000 and you are a higher-rate taxpayer you will save €980. A lower-rate income taxpayer will save €580. And the scheme is only available to employees, which excludes the self-employed and contractors.*

 SOME THINGS TO WATCH OUT FOR *If you lose a Leap card you should be able to get it replaced at no cost as long as you have registered it on www.leapcard.ie. If it is stolen you will need to have it blocked. But if your Taxsaver ticket is not in the form of a Leap card, it will cost you €15 to replace an annual or monthly ticket issued by Iarnród Éireann. Bus Éireann uses Leap cards that are replaced through www.leapcard.ie. For lost/stolen point-to-point tickets there is a €15 replacement charge. The same cost applies to Dublin Bus and Luas when tickets need to be replaced.*

 USEFUL WEBSITES *For more information on Taxsaver, see www.taxsaver. ie/Commuters.*

Information on the Leap card scheme is at https://about.leapcard.ie/.

29

BROADBAND

TOPIC/SUBJECT	Lifestyle
EXPECTED SAVINGS OR EARNINGS	Around €300 if you switch to a bundle with an introductory discount
TIME REQUIRED	1 hour
LEVEL OF DIFFICULTY	● ● ● ○ ○

There is plenty of competition in the broadband market, assuming you can get decent coverage in your area. And if you are prepared to bundle your broadband provision with television and telephone services, you can really save a packet. A bundled service is usually cheaper as operators have you locked in for a far higher monthly spend than if you only sign up for one service. Like electricity and gas suppliers, you normally need to sign up for at least a year to get the best deals, accept electronic billing, and pay by direct debit from your bank's current account, according to price comparison site www.bonkers.ie.

WHERE THE PROBLEM LIES

Our old friend inertia means we often sign up for a broadband service, and if we are happy with it, we stick with it even though we could probably do better by moving to another operator. This is a pity because we have a vibrant market in Ireland for internet, telephone and TV services, with deals aplenty.

You could also be paying for a service you no longer need. More and more people are watching TV online, via streaming services. If this is how you watch your TV, it would be worth considering whether to cancel your TV subscription, and instead go for a broadband-only deal, according to comparison site www.switcher.ie.

And research commissioned by Switcher has found that Irish TV customers have an average of 155 channels but the majority watch less than a quarter of what they pay for. We sit and watch an average of 13 hours of TV a week. One in five people actually watches 21 hours or more of TV every week. Most of us return to the same channels again and again. What all this indicates is that the TV packages we are paying for might not be the right ones for our viewing habits or needs.

The findings suggest that households could be wasting money on services they are not using. The standard (non-discounted) cost of TV packages ranges from over €350 to €1,000 a year. But just 2% of customers say they watch more than three-quarters of the channels they pay for, while one in ten watches between half and three-quarters.

HOW TO FIX IT

Checking out the market for the deals on offer can be complicated. Do a search online putting in the word 'broadband' and a plethora of websites of individual service providers pop up. They try hard to reel you in, but it can be difficult to know what is a good deal and what is a stinker.

A better bet might be to use price comparison websites such as Bonkers or Switcher.

Some of the key factors to consider regarding broadband and digital TV packages, according to Switcher, include the following:

- the quality of broadband service regarding speed and download allowance

- how many channels are available
- the cost of installation (if applicable)
- the cost of a set-top box (if applicable)
- how long the contract is for
- any additional landline costs.

For broadband, research by Switcher shows that cost and speed are the two biggest factors at play when people decide to switch, so it's worth taking time to look at these elements.

Unlimited broadband will be really important for people in a busy household or shared accommodation – it means that the bill will be the same each month, regardless of how much data you use.

Note also that there are many teaser deals out there. This is where you get a hugely discounted deal, or free add-ons, like Netflix, for six months. Some providers also offer things like cash-back, free TVs or prepaid credit cards to new customers. It is important to look beyond the period of a discount deal, and freebies, and see what you will pay over a year.

This includes a satellite dish to receive the UK channels – though if you already have a Sky dish, you can use that – and an aerial for the Irish ones, as well as a set-top combibox to control them.

How to switch
Check what the best price options are. The regulator ComReg (Commission for Communications Regulation) has a website, callcosts. ie, where you can enter details of your phone and broadband usage to see how different packages compare.

Bonkers and Switcher make the job of comparing deals very easy. They outline details of stand-alone TV packages as well as bundled offers with phone and broadband.

Check you don't still have months left to run on your contract or you could face early-exit penalties, which are sometimes as high as paying off the remainder of your contract. Contact your provider if you are not sure. Remember, you'll also need to make sure you give your current broadband and TV provider(s) the specified notice to cancel your current contract to ensure that you're not charged after you've switched provider – even if you're outside the minimum term of your contract. And you'll need to cancel any direct debits you have with your current provider, too.

If you do find a better offer from a new provider, it is worth contacting the old one to see if they can match it or give you a better deal to keep your custom. If you do decide to switch, you'll need to get your universal account number from your phone bill – you'll need to give this to your new provider. Contact your new provider by phone or online and they will switch you at an appointed date and send out any new equipment necessary. Your old provider may come to pick up equipment after you have cancelled with them.

THE SAVINGS EXPLAINED

You can waste a truckload of money on your broadband service by having the wrong deal. Switching is easy and there are plenty of great introductory offers available that can radically reduce your bill. Before you sign up for another deal, it is essential to ensure you have the right type of package.

You may be a light broadband user, which means you should consider a cheaper, capped service. On the other hand, if you and your family are heavy users, an unlimited allowance could save you money – many fibre providers now offer unlimited deals. Of course, in terms of broadband, where you live could greatly impact the type of connection you could get. People in rural areas are potentially limited to satellite or mobile broadband. But shopping around can still get you a good deal on these services.

It is worth noting that if your existing broadband, telephone or TV service provider notifies you that it is raising the price it charges, you can break out of your contract without incurring a financial penalty. This is because a price rise amounts to a significant change in the terms and conditions of your contract. But you need to act with 30 days of getting notice of the price increase.

TIME *It should take you no more than an hour to move to a new provider, whether for broadband on its own, or for a bundle of services.*

 DIFFICULTY *This one is easy-peasy, especially if you use one of the price comparison sites we have recommended.*

 SOME THINGS TO WATCH OUT FOR *The majority of TV plans come with features like the ability to pause, rewind and record TV, while Eir, Virgin Media and Sky also have apps that allow you to watch TV on the move. Sky and Virgin Media also have a huge amount of on-demand content for customers, which can be appealing, as more of us watch TV when we want, rather than following traditional viewing schedules. If you do want to stream, you will need a good internet connection. Broadband-only plans with speeds up to 360Mb are available with low introductory prices, so you could save by opting for a broadband-only deal if you're sure you don't want the TV with it. Some providers also offer free Netflix for the first six months of your TV contract, or cash-back when you sign up.*

 USEFUL WEBSITES *The Commission for Communications Regulation (ComReg) has a useful price comparison site with a frequently asked questions section at www.callcosts.ie.*

Price comparison sites www.bonkers.ie and www.switcher.ie are even easier to use. They do not charge for the information they provide, but do earn commission if you take out a service by linking to a provider from their sites.

30
DENTAL EXPENSES

TOPIC/SUBJECT	Medical expenses
EXPECTED SAVINGS OR EARNINGS	€300
TIME REQUIRED	4 hours
LEVEL OF DIFFICULTY	●●●○○

For many, going to the dentist is daunting – emotionally, physically and financially. People often put off a visit to the dentist because they are scared, but the sheer cost of having work done on our teeth can also be a huge disincentive. This means people often avoid sitting in the dentist's chair until they reach the stage where they need a lot of work done, a point at which the treatment that needs to be undertaken is then costly.

WHERE THE PROBLEM LIES

A trip to the dentist is no one's idea of fun, and it can also extract a lot of dosh from your pocket. But there are options to dull the financial pain. The Dental Treatment Scheme covers the cost of some treatments for those paying PRSI (pay related social insurance) in work and retired people with sufficient contributions. Other options include going outside this jurisdiction.

HOW TO FIX IT

There are a number of ways you can lessen the impact of the cost of having dental work done. These include having some of the cost covered by the State's Dental Treatment Services Scheme, paying for treatment outside the country, getting the Department of Social Protection (DSP) in the Republic to reimburse you for work done abroad, putting a dental insurance plan in place, availing of tax relief, and using a payment plan at your dental surgery.

Dental Treatment Services Scheme

This is a scheme run by the Department of Social Protection (DPS) that provides dental, optical and aural services to qualified people. It is available to workers and retired people who have the required number of PRSI contributions.

Medical card holders are entitled to more extensive dental, ophthalmic and aural services from the HSE, but in practice the availability of these services varies from area to area. The treatment scheme was extended to self-employed people in 2016 if they have paid sufficient Class S PRSI contributions.

Those on the medical card fare the best in terms of free benefits; they are entitled to an annual check-up, two fillings, unlimited extractions and emergency pain treatment.

PAYE workers are only allowed one check-up before they have to pay.

HSE dental clinics provide services for children of school-going age. This service is accessed through screening appointments in your child's primary school.

Paying for treatment outside the country

Dental tourism has become popular since the economy here hit the skids in 2008. Dental tourism is when patients from one country visit another for dental care, typically because it is cheaper. Northern Ireland is a popular place for treatment, but so too are Eastern European countries.

Many parents take children across the border to have braces fitted, which works out far cheaper than identical work in the Republic.

Costs vary hugely depending on which jurisdiction you get the dental work done in. Take root-canal work. It ranges from €425 to €1,000 in Ireland, but in Newry prices range from €260 to €360. In some Eastern European countries the same work costs €100. Implants will set you back up to €2,500 in Ireland. Up North you can get an implant, which will involve a number of visits, for €2,000. In Budapest you can pay as little as €500, with this procedure often costing €1,000.

Treatment benefits in the EU

If you choose to have treatment in another EU member state, the DSP will pay an amount equivalent to the rate paid for similar treatments carried out in Ireland. Alternatively, it will pay the amount actually paid for the treatment, whichever is the lower. You must still have the qualifying PRSI contributions.

Contact the Treatment Benefit Section before you travel to get an application form and details of the amounts the department will pay.

In 2016, 35 claims amounting to €1,122 were received. Most of these were Northern Ireland-based and mainly down to geography and practicality, according to the department.

The arrangements for customers to obtain reimbursement in respect of treatment benefit services provided in another EU member state precedes the EU Directive 201/24 and the Cross-Border Healthcare Directive.

Tax relief

Tax relief is allowed on some dental treatments, but some of the most common procedures are excluded, namely extractions, fillings and cleaning. The tax relief is at the standard rate of 20%. However, the tax relief does cover some of the most expensive procedures, such as crowns, implants and root-canal work. You need to fill out form MED 2 from Revenue, and you can claim for the previous four years.

Dental insurance

You may have health insurance, but policies often do not cover dental treatments. Those policies that offer cover for what are called day-to-day medical expenses will reimburse you for some of the costs of a dental procedure, as well as the likes of GP costs. Another option is a specific dental insurance plan. Dental cover helps you manage the high cost of routine dental treatment. Most of these stand-alone plans provide immediate cover for check-ups, cleaning and emergency treatment immediately following an accident or injury. They include benefits for minor treatments such as fillings or extractions, and some of the higher-level plans include benefits for major treatments such as crowns and orthodontics (for children), according to health insurance broker Dermot Goode of Total Health Cover. Remember that policies often carry an excess (an amount of the claim you have to pay), and there may be an annual limit you can claim.

Payment plans

Many larger dental practices offer structured payment plans for ongoing treatments. Do ask about this as they may let you pay monthly, which will ease the burden a little.

THE SAVINGS EXPLAINED

The different schemes and options to help you save money when it comes to having dental work carried out have been outlined above.

TIME *Investigating the various means to help you cover the cost of dental work is time-consuming, but may be well worth it. Do lots of research before taking any of the options outlined here, and make sure to contact the DSP before having work done outside the State that you hope to be reimbursed for when you return.*

DIFFICULTY *It is not hugely difficult to work out the best options to defray some of the cost of dental work, but you will need to focus hard on it. Set aside an afternoon to work out how to tackle the task. It may be well worth it – to your pocket and your mouth – in the end.*

SOME THINGS TO WATCH OUT FOR *The DSP may quibble, or even refuse to stump up the funds if you go outside the jurisdiction to have work done. So get as much advance clearance as possible. Consider how much follow-up care you will need. Is it worth it to fly to Budapest for a tooth implant when several visits are required, and what if something goes wrong after the initial work has been done? Also consider the cost of a dental insurance plan. Ask yourself how often you visit the dentist. If you have good teeth you may not need to pay into a plan.*

 USEFUL WEBSITES *For details on dental treatment benefits abroad, see the DSP's website at www.welfare.ie/en/Pages/Treatment-Benefit1.aspx.*

31

CAR CARE AND FUEL

TOPIC/SUBJECT	Transport
EXPECTED SAVINGS OR EARNINGS	€390
TIME REQUIRED	1 hour
LEVEL OF DIFFICULTY	● ○ ○ ○ ○

If you own a vehicle, whether it's a car, a motorbike or anything with an engine, you are supporting all manner of costs. In other chapters we are looking at things like insurance and other incidental costs, but something you may not be thinking of regularly is the benefit of simple maintenance and the cost that not doing it incurs.

We'll assume that you spend about €50 a week on fuel. This may be above or below what you actually use – you can adjust the figure according to your own situation. If you fit our example you are spending €2,600 a year on fuel.

What many of us don't realise is that there are factors that will increase your fuel consumption (you'll get less mileage out of the same amount of fuel), either because of how you drive or because of certain aspects of the vehicle you use.

WHERE THE PROBLEM LIES

When was the last time you checked your tyre pressure? During winter months the cold air contracts and your tyre can lose a few pounds of pressure. Did you know that not having your tyres properly inflated can make you lose about 5–10% fuel efficiency? A study carried out in the USA by Carnegie University put the figure even higher, at 20%. That means that for every €20 you put in you are throwing away anything from €1 to €4 for no good reason at all.

Some estimates say that keeping your engine tuned makes a difference of 4% to your fuel consumption. That's about €1 for every €20 you spend.

That's before we look at 'how you drive', which is another big factor.

HOW TO FIX IT

Some of this is as easy as going into a petrol station and taking five minutes to check your tyre pressure and top them up accordingly. Keep your annual check-ups or the mileage-based ones that your mechanic or garage advises you to do. When it comes to motors an ounce of prevention is usually better than a pound of cure.

How you drive also matters. If you drive fast it can be dangerous – particularly in poor driving conditions – but it will also cost you more. Accelerating a lot or inefficient driving (going from fast to slow a lot) uses more fuel. In the same way, hitting the brakes a lot means that your vehicle loses momentum. If you are driving sensibly you don't need to go from high to low speeds a lot. That is before we consider the additional costs of this to things like your brake pads and discs.

Driving with your windows down is also a fuel burner as it creates more drag. Another thing people do unawares is keeping things like storage boxes or racks on their car when they are not in use for months at a time. That may be handy for when you do use them, but it's definitely being paid for several times in the process by creating more drag.

Getting your air filter changed at tune-ups is cheap, and a dirty filter can lower your fuel efficiency, as can using air conditioning.

One of the advantages of smartphones is that you can use them to find the cheapest fuel prices. Petrol prices vary by up to 5% based on where you buy the fuel. A phone app like Pumps.ie will give you prices and the geolocation so that you can get the best deals around.

THE SAVINGS EXPLAINED

If we take it that your tyres aren't fully filled, you've skipped car tuning, and there are some other factors affecting your vehicle's fuel efficiency, such as the way you drive, you'd be paying 2% more for fuel than you could have, then we can deduce that savings of about 15% are possible.

The best thing of all is that most of these money-saving tips are painless and nearly costless to implement. Fuel apps are free, as is getting your tyre pressure right – anybody can do these things.

Use your own situation to figure out your own potential savings, but if you are in the €50 per week camp you could save up to €390 a year, or just over a euro a day, on costs associated with fuel purchase. This is not something you want to drive by (forgive the pun).

 TIME *It doesn't take long at all to take care of something correctly, but it takes far longer after a bit of mild neglect means it breaks or requires repair. The old saying 'a stitch in time saves nine' is very true with mechanical things generally. About two hours a year spent sensibly will take care of most of this.*

 DIFFICULTY *It's easy to inflate a tyre and it's easy to get your car checked at one of the many places across the country. What isn't always so easy is remembering that while your car will still work if you skip this, in time, you'll pay for it. Maintenance is way underrated.*

SOME THINGS TO WATCH OUT FOR *Obviously you don't want to overdo it. If you get your car's computer read (if it has one), you'll always find errors on it, many of which have no material impact on the car at all and it is uneconomic to fix them because they are so minor. So don't get caught up in trying to have every last thing perfect. Just do your best to have it as good as you can at a reasonable price.*

 USEFUL WEBSITES
www.pumps.ie
http://www.carbibles.com/gasmileage.html
www.rsa.ie
http://www.wikihow.com/Increase-Fuel-Mileage-on-a-Car

32

HOUSE-SWAP HOLIDAYS

TOPIC/SUBJECT	Holidays
EXPECTED SAVINGS OR EARNINGS	€1,100
TIME REQUIRED	6 hours
LEVEL OF DIFFICULTY	● ● ● ○ ○

Like many people, Charlie and I both like to take the odd break. Charlie likes to go to France, I'm more into Spain, but that hardly matters because what we both learn every year is that escaping the Irish summer for the continent is never cheap. It doesn't seem to matter what you do or who you fly with, holidays are expensive.

So in this chapter we are going to look at an idea that a lot of people have used for 'cost mitigation'. The idea is a house-swap.

WHERE THE PROBLEM LIES

When you go away, particularly if you have kids, you may find you start to lean towards nicer accommodation or places where you can self-cater; and this has led to a big surge in people staying in other people's homes. Services like Owners Direct and Airbnb give you this type of accommodation for a fee, but there are others through which you can get the same thing for much less.

If you look at any decent property in a decent location you can expect to pay between €50 and €200 a day (depending on the country and the region in that country). If you were to go away for ten days you could easily end up with a cost of €1,500 on top of flights, car rental and spending money.

This is a large part of what makes a holiday pricey, but it doesn't have to be that way.

HOW TO FIX IT

When you go abroad, the chances are your house will be empty, so why not use it as a form of collateral against a home in the place you are going to? This is where house-swaps come into play.

If you do a house-swap you find people somewhere else with a comparable property and you quite literally 'swap homes' and pay the broker service (be it a person or a website) a small fee for arranging things.

Doing this comes with a lot of advantages. You can often get somewhere in a nice location that is suited to a family, and you have the whole house rather than a hotel room or two. Some people with pets do swaps with other pet-owners so that they don't have to arrange kennels or organise somebody to care for their pets.

If you have children it is common enough for the families to leave out some toys that the visitors can play with, and vice versa, so that your kids aren't bored out of their minds if you have a few rainy days when you get there.

There is a downside: you can't book whenever you want; there needs to be a counterparty who wants to do the swap at the same time. You also have to have some faith in humanity, because obviously the visitors could choose to look through your drawers, so being comfortable with strangers in your house is a prerequisite.

That said, the people Karl has spoken to who do it have all given rave reviews about how well it has worked out. He has spoken to families who have swapped their house here in Ireland for homes in Europe, Australia and South America.

It pays to do your own due diligence. Look up the location on a satellite map and see if you can get a street view. Find out if the person has done this before and what other people who stayed in the property thought of it.

There is a risk to this, but the upside is that you can usually save some serious money (see below), and in many cases people make friends with locals, or the people they swapped with, and have very positive experiences.

THE SAVINGS EXPLAINED

Go to any website and see how much a hotel would cost for a family for ten days or two weeks. Then compare that with a B&B or a house rental, be it one on AirBnB or anywhere else.

Then take the cost of this (which we are assuming will be at least €1,300) and compare that to the cost of doing a house-swap – the price is typically an annual membership in the region of €100–200.

Take the €1,300 cost, subtract the house-swap cost, and you are up by about €1,100. By the law of averages, you'll have a lovely time in a nice house and when you get home your own gaff won't be wrecked.

 TIME *It takes a little time to organise a swap, to research the area, and then to make your house 'visitor ready'. Sometimes it's a quick process, other times it can be slow, as much of it depends on what you are trying to do or where you are going.*

 DIFFICULTY *It's not that difficult, but it does take some trust and preparation. Because we estimate about six hours, it warrants three stars.*

SOME THINGS TO WATCH OUT FOR *Make sure you use a reputable site, make sure you are happy with the people you are swapping with and do your homework. Preparation is key.*

 USEFUL WEBSITES
www.homeexchange.com
https://homelink.org
www.exchangezones.com/Europe-Home-Exchange.htm
www.intervac.com

33

HAND-
ME-DOWN
CLOTHES

TOPIC/SUBJECT	Household spending
EXPECTED SAVINGS OR EARNINGS	€240
TIME REQUIRED	1 hour
LEVEL OF DIFFICULTY	● ○ ○ ○ ○

Children's clothes are very affordable these days, but anything of high quality still tends to be expensive. That rule is fairly consistent across many things in life.

Children will typically be harder on clothes than adults (things like workwear aside). Add to this the fact that children grow and frequently need new clothes, so even if you get them the best clothes they won't last because they just outgrow everything.

It all adds up. Factor in things like sports gear and school uniforms and you could be looking at six or more full sets of clothing in a year, plus two or three pairs of shoes and perhaps a winter coat.

If you spend on average about €40 for a full set of clothing per child, you'll go through €240 per child per year (not including shoes).

Multiply that number by the number of children in your house and it can get big quickly. For this tip we'll assume that you have two children; but as with every chapter in this book, you can adjust the figures up or down to suit your own situation.

Obviously, if you buy all clothes at a discount shop you will spend less, but few people stick to that strictly and end up buying a mixture of low-cost and more expensive clothes.

WHERE THE PROBLEM LIES
Parents feel pressure to have their children kitted out in nice clothes, and while we are certainly not going to tell you how to dress your children, there are things you can do to lower the cost. For a start, don't compete. There are always going to be people who have nicer things, including nicer clothes for their kids. Somebody somewhere will always be richer than you, have a smarter car or whatever it might be.

Some children are more into fashion than others (Charlie has teenage daughters and is now well versed in this), and there are also children who become very brand conscious at a very young age, and all of this can result in higher outgoings on clothing.

HOW TO FIX IT
Get into the habit of swapping clothes or passing them on. That we have clothes banks across the country is in part testament to the fact that we probably don't do enough of this.

There are local groups on Facebook where people put things up for 'sale or swap', but the most obvious place to start is a group of your own peers or of parents of children older than your own who may be a ready source of clothes.

If somebody is going to send their stuff to a clothes bank, what harm is it to ask if they might consider letting you use the same thing? Let it be known that you could use clothes. There are also people who are thoughtful enough to ask if you'd like some clothes their own kids won't be using again.

There is a fine line between doing this the right way and in a polite manner versus being a weirdo about it, so get the balance right, and remember to reciprocate – you can't expect people to give if you don't do the same. If the person helping you out won't be taking clothes back because their kids will always, by virtue of them being older than yours, be too big for things you might have, try to find some other thing you can do to make up for it.

THE SAVINGS EXPLAINED

If you can reduce the expenditure per child by say, three to four sets of clothes (not including underwear/socks/shoes) and are able to get good-quality hand-me-down clothes, you can offset some of your expenditure. Often people are more diligent about passing on the 'good' things they have bought (more so than a cheap T-shirt, for instance) so it may be that the 'value' is greater than the €40 we mentioned above.

We'll assume that you can save three full sets of clothes, or €120 per child per year, which in our example comes to €240 per year.

 TIME *It doesn't take too long to sort through clothes – assuming you have a source of second-hand clothing.*

 DIFFICULTY *Easy: you just keep the things you like and either return or donate the things that you don't like (but make sure to agree this with the person who gives you the clothing).*

 SOMETHINGS TO WATCH OUT FOR *Try to reciprocate in some way if you have a person who helps you out continuously. A good source of clothing can morph into a lost friendship if it's all one-way.*

 USEFUL WEBSITES
www.facebook.com

34

RECYCLING

TOPIC/SUBJECT	Household spending
EXPECTED SAVINGS OR EARNINGS	€210
TIME REQUIRED	Depends, but about 1 hour versus what you already do anyway
LEVEL OF DIFFICULTY	● ○ ○ ○ ○

Recycling and being thrifty with your waste is something that many older people will relate to, in particular if they grew up experiencing rationing during the Second World War.

For the rest of us recycling isn't about keeping something because you might not get it again (the waste not, want not approach), it's more about environmental impact and being a responsible citizen. While this is an admirable ambition, it wasn't until we started to be charged for waste and bins that it truly made a difference and compelled people to make better decisions.

Think about where you live prior to the plastic bag levy. In fact, look at some old pictures and the chances are you'll see a plastic bag in the background somewhere. Introducing a 22c fee eradicated an endemic problem almost overnight.

As the cost of waste rises (via taxes and landfill fees) it becomes more financially sensible to throw out at little as possible and to embrace the 'three Rs' – reduce, reuse and recycle.

WHERE THE PROBLEM LIES

Sometimes it's more convenient to throw things away. If you're away from home, maybe going for a walk, and you buy some crisps, will you carry that wrapper all the way home to recycle it or throw it in a local bin where it probably won't be recycled?

The green bin doesn't take glass bottles and for this reason many of us don't recycle glass. This is a real pity because in other countries it's done so well that you don't see anywhere near the level of waste that we have in Ireland by not having bottle collections done correctly.

If you ever go to Germany, for instance, you'll see people going back to the off licence with a crate of empties to collect the rebate on them. While it would be great to see that happen here, it probably won't any time soon. You're expected to bring your bottles to the bottle bank – wouldn't it be a start to have a bottle collection instead?

Sometimes it's understandable not to recycle, but it's a bad financial decision if you don't recycle all you can. Every time you throw something in the bin that could be recycled you are almost literally throwing money away.

The pay-by-weight system is on the way countrywide; so in the future you'll pay the price for how you dispose of things.

HOW TO FIX IT

The first thing to do is have a procedure for separating waste. Many households have different bins for doing this. The general waste bin (often the 'black bin', but it can be any colour depending on where you live and who does your collection) is for things that can't go into the 'green bin' (recyclables) or the 'brown bin' (food waste), if you have one.

Many areas have a set charge for making a bin collection available. This is the quarterly standing charge. Then there is a 'pay per lift', which tends to be lower or zero for the recyclables and food waste bins.

If you don't manage this in any way and just throw everything into the general waste bin, you will be paying over the odds. Some companies, such as City Bin, give their customers reports showing how much they recycle versus other customers, and that helps to give you an idea if you are above or below average.

If you're below average, make the change and you'll be better off for it. Our current recycling rate is 45%, but it is hoped that by 2020 we will reach a national average of 50%.

In Ireland we are good about recycling, the third best in Europe in fact, but on the other hand we produce a lot of waste. According to the European Commission the Irish generate the fourth highest waste per person in the EU at 623kg per person. So we do a good job of being 'green', but we still have a lot of waste.

THE SAVINGS EXPLAINED

If you reuse bags, such as cloth bags, or the more durable ones available at any supermarket, you can shave a euro off your weekly shopping every week. That gives you about €50 a year. You can use any bags you do end up buying for bins in your bathroom or kitchen, or reuse them in some other way if you can. The main thing is not to just turf them out; keep them until you can put them to good use a second time.

On bins, if we assume that you don't do much in the way of recycling and that you miss out on recycling about 2kg of waste a week, that adds up to 104kg a year per person. If you are in a household of four people that's about 400kg or more per year that doesn't have to go in the bin. If the average landfill bin is filled using about 25kg of waste, you will use the bin 16 times more in a year than required.

Next, figure out your price per bin lift. We'll assume it's around €10 a time, so not recycling costs our fictitious household €160 a year.

If you are going to throw something out anyway, it's not that big a deal to segregate the waste. You may need to get a second bin in your kitchen (where most of the waste originates) or to move your bins somewhere close to a back door or patio if you are worried about smells, etc.

It may take a few small changes, but reusing bags and recycling are well worth it because with savings of €210 on the line it is throwing money away if you don't adjust how you do things.

 TIME *Virtually no time – just whatever time it takes to put different things in different bins.*

 DIFFICULTY *Almost none. Just do what you are going to do anyway, but change where things end up.*

 SOME THINGS TO WATCH OUT FOR *Stay diligent. A plan like this requires you to follow through to see the savings.*

 USEFUL WEBSITES
www.stopfoodwaste.ie
www.repak.ie/for-consumers/facilities-search/
www.brownbin.ie

35

LOSE
WEIGHT

TOPIC/SUBJECT	Lifestyle
EXPECTED SAVINGS OR EARNINGS	€600
TIME REQUIRED	Days/weeks/months of ongoing commitment
LEVEL OF DIFFICULTY	● ● ● ● ○

It was unlikely that we'd get through any serious book on being better off financially without offending anybody, and this chapter will do it for many of us. Frankly, we are a nation of fatties and it's time to trim down, if not for your personal health then at least for your financial wellbeing.

This matters because the Irish are the second most obese people in the entire Organisation for Economic Co-operation and Development – that means we're one away from the top slot out of 32 countries, being pipped to first place by Malta. Our rate of obesity is 23%, which is more than double what it was in the year 2000.

Every fourth person reading this is technically obese and about every second person is overweight. The costs of this are tricky to determine, but they are 'real' costs to the individual and to society at large.

In the UK the annual cost of obesity was in 2008 estimated to be £8 billion per year – it could well be higher now. In Ireland we have yet to calculate these costs, but as we are more obese than people in the UK, the chances are that the cost per person is higher.

To temper this, we should make it clear that the problem isn't just a home-grown one. Worldwide, obesity has doubled since 1980. Globally, more people die from being overweight than from being underweight, something that we rarely hear.

Contrary to what we might think, half of the obese children below the age of five aren't in the USA or Europe, but in Asia, the very place where traditional diets virtually guaranteed that people were fairly lean in the past.

WHERE THE PROBLEM LIES

If you're obese there are higher odds that you will die younger. It is therefore an 'anti-wealth' aspect of life, similar in many ways to smoking.

Obviously there are people who are obese or who smoke who live to be a hundred, but they are the rarity. The health issues (which are costly to work with if you get any of them and survive) are things like diabetes, heart disease, stroke and several different forms of cancer.

These are all non-communicable diseases – you don't 'catch' them, you bestow them on yourself. Obesity is quickly taking over smoking as the leading cause of preventable cancer.

According to the American College of Occupational Medicine, obesity adds more to healthcare costs than smoking and those who are morbidly obese (which in general means being 100lb over your ideal weight) are almost three times more costly than smokers.

The cures are in the food we eat. It's just as Hippocrates said a few thousand years ago: 'Let food be thy medicine and medicine be thy food.' If you eat lots of sugar and fats and go over your calorie requirement you'll gain weight. If you stay on that path you will become overweight and eventually obese.

We're not calling for fat shaming, but we'll be damned if we'll go so far as to say 'It's okay'. Being obese isn't any more 'okay' than smoking is 'okay'. Call it like it is – it results from a bad set of choices that should be reversed where possible.

Financially, it's a disaster waiting to happen. If you die prematurely you take time away from yourself, from your loved ones being able to spend time with you and from your capacity to earn and have a longer, healthier life. Days of work are lost, health outcomes are lower – these are actual 'costs' which need to be counted.

Not calling out the issue of weight is like saying it's okay to choose not to address debt issues. This isn't the same as 'fat shaming' – we aren't saying you should be ashamed – but you also can't live in denial of reality. The government doesn't have the resolve to tax actual obesity, so it will try to tax sugar instead, which punishes everybody, including those who aren't adding to the healthcare burden by not being obese.

Losing weight isn't easy to do – and both of your authors could do with slimming down a little.

HOW TO FIX IT

The weight loss industry is a multi-billion-euro industry the world over. If there was an easy fix, we wouldn't have any obesity. It's unlikely that anybody, given the choice, would choose to be obese. Time and regular good food choices are important factors. Your general wealth level also counts: the less well off you are, the more likely you are to be overweight.

Dr Melanie Lührmann, a health economist in the UK, did some interesting research that revealed that we eat less now in terms of calories than we did in the year 1980. We are spending more time exercising too! Not only that, we are eating better food and less sugar, and we are also drinking less alcohol.

Despite this, obesity rates are rising. The main issue she identified is that we don't work in jobs as physical as the ones we used to do. More people sit at computers or desks now than they used to, and this means adjusting calorie intake downwards and ramping up exercise a little more.

Her research also looked at how people keep food diaries. No surprises here – the majority of people lie. So one of the first fixes is that you have to be honest, not with others, but with yourself.

If you are a parent or want to be better off, look at your kids or your bank balance and if you are carrying too much weight, ask yourself, 'Should I trim down or deprive myself of time with loved ones and better wealth?'

Why have a doughnut on your plate when you could add it as a zero to your bank balance? The fix is simple. You'll need to track what you eat: use an app on your phone if you have a smartphone, and be honest with yourself. Figure out ways to eat more nutrient-dense food, avoid junk, avoid sugar, have a goal and on the journey (which is hard) have some milestones, then bask in the glow of somebody you haven't seen in a while noticing and telling you how much better you look.

THE SAVINGS EXPLAINED

If the UK cost is £8 billion and their population is 64 million with an obesity rate not too far off ours, this means that approximately 13 million people are behind that £8 billion cost. This breaks down to a cost of £615 per year per person who is obese.

If we assume that costs are similar here, it's safe to say that our figure of €600 per year is fair. Naturally, not all of this is borne by the obese person themselves; some of it is covered by the welfare system, the health system and other aspects of our social protections.

Equally, if you are shaving years off your life, this is difficult to put a financial value on in the here and now. So while deflected costs will lower the figure from €600 downwards, it should be raised to account for shorter lifespan and the direct costs in the future of higher chances of non-communicable disease. For that reason we'll leave the figure at €600. Trim down enough and you'll be better off in more ways than one; you'll have higher odds of a longer, healthier life and spend less time with health complications.

The one caveat: don't go to the point of developing an eating disorder.

 TIME *A diet and/or exercise-based approach to weight loss is highly effective, but it does take time as you have to make the right decisions again and again. Eating badly, on the other hand, is always easy and convenient. Then there is the time it takes to exercise, to prepare meals and all of the other time-consuming things that go with it.*

DIFFICULTY *We know this one is hard because... well, just ask anybody. Very few people will tell you it's very easy to stay trim. Commitment to a plan like this requires discipline and the capacity to stay on track when falling off the wagon is so easy.*

 SOME THINGS TO WATCH OUT FOR *If you do start to keep a food diary, don't lie to yourself. The more honest you are the more you'll understand what you are doing right and wrong. Also, try to find some kind of healthy treat which you can snack on. Everybody needs a little something to sin with, but if you go for an old reliable like crisps or chocolate, you can undo a whole week's worth of cut calories in a few minutes.*

 USEFUL WEBSITES *www.mynetdiary.com is a great app for food tracking. Karl used it to lose about 15% of his body weight back in 2016 and again in 2017.*
www.fitbit.com
www.weightwatchers.ie
www.diabetes.ie

36

CHANGE THE LIGHTS

TOPIC/SUBJECT	Household spending
EXPECTED SAVINGS OR EARNINGS	€65
TIME REQUIRED	1 hour
LEVEL OF DIFFICULTY	● ○ ○ ○ ○

Energy is one of the key components of any economy. Energy, or lack of it, can cause every manner of problem, from food shortages to wars.

In Ireland recent reports by the Sustainable Energy Authority of Ireland (SEAI) have shown that electricity consumption is up almost 3% a year. In Chapter 10 we discussed energy providers; this chapter is about how you use energy.

The carbon intensity of electricity has fallen by nearly half since 1990, to a low of 456g CO_2/kWh in 2014. In 2015 it increased by 2.5% as a result of the near 20% increase in coal used for generation. So while we are getting 'greener' in many ways, the pollution caused by energy creation is still a big factor, and as that gets taxed more you can see costs rise or stay stagnant even when commodity prices drop.

Lighting is a massive part of energy consumption. In the USA the Energy Information Administration estimates that 10% of all residential energy is used in lighting.

In Ireland we categorise energy in a different way. 'Primary energy' is the energy used in buildings, most of which is used for lighting, heating or cooling a building. In 2015, primary energy in buildings accounted for 39% of energy supply. Overall, primary energy use in buildings has increased by 20% since 1990. In 2015 it grew by 3.3%.

WHERE THE PROBLEM LIES

So many things we use are chipping away at your wealth. While people might go to some lengths to buy an energy-efficient microwave or vacuum cleaner, do you think about the things in your house that are on for long periods of time?

Freezers and fridges come into that category; so do lights. In particular, during an Irish winter you'll have lights on for long periods of time. If you don't have energy-efficient appliances or lights you will use more electricity and in turn pay out more than you should.

Leaving lights on, for instance in a hallway, an empty room, or an outside porch, is using electricity that doesn't have to be used. Or in any case, it doesn't have to be used at the *rate* it is being used because there are more efficient options out there that enable you to get the same effect more cheaply.

So if you like having a light on the door to your house, make sure it isn't a 100 watt regular bulb when it could be a 10 watt energy-efficient one.

HOW TO FIX IT

This will take a little expenditure, but it will make a difference. The first thing you can do is start to replace light bulbs. The third-generation LED lights out now are great, even downlighters (the first energy-efficient ones weren't very bright).

They also come with different light colours, so you aren't stuck with the cold blue/white light early editions had. They now come in warmer yellows, which are more like the light traditional bulbs gave out.

Replacing the lights is so simple that if you haven't already done it you ought to be asking yourself why.

THE SAVINGS EXPLAINED

Compact fluorescent lamps (CFLs) use 80% less electricity than regular bulbs. They also last up to ten times longer. According to the Sustainable Energy Authority of Ireland, replacing three conventional light bulbs with CFLs can save a household up to €37 per annum.

If you want to get more precise you can work out the kilowatt hours being used before and after you replace the bulbs and determine a more precise figure, but we are happy to go with the SEAI's estimate. Better yet, check out Electric Ireland's lighting calculator (see the Useful Websites below) – you choose the number of lights you have, what you are going to replace the bulbs with, the average hours a day they are used, and it will give you your savings to the nearest cent.

While we don't have exact figures for what people are using, we can make certain assumptions about the number of bulbs in an average house. Often people have a hallway, at least two bedrooms, a sitting or living room, a kitchen and one or two bathrooms. For this reason we can hazard a guess that you'll have at least six light bulbs that can be replaced.

But the savings don't come for free; you have to buy the bulbs. If you go online you can find LED bulbs for as little as €1.50 each. This is a saving of about 50% on what they cost in the shops. This means replacing your six bulbs will cost nearer €9 than €18. There is a saving there, but also an outlay, so we have to put the money spent against the money saved. You can save €74 but you had to spend €9 to get it, so the net saving is €65.

A few other points worth noting are that dirt can reduce lamp efficiency by up to 25%; common sense tips like turning off lights when you leave a room and the like are also important.

If you have low energy-efficiency appliances, then when you do get around to replacing them be sure to get something that is A+ rated. We hope we'll save you enough that you can afford a new appliance if you need one, but unlike lights, the outlay on a new fridge can be such that replacing it instantly may not be the best idea.

 TIME *At one hour or less, this is a 'quick fix' idea that takes very little time.*

 DIFFICULTY *Other than having to shell out for new lights, it's easy – even a DIY luddite can do it.*

 SOME THINGS TO WATCH OUT FOR *There are different types of energy-saving lights and different types of attachments (some have pins, others screw in). Just make sure you are buying compatible types and also remember that different generations of LED have different features. The new ones have a better 'natural light' effect while the older ones are often more 'blue' looking.*

 USEFUL WEBSITES
www.seai.ie
www.electricireland.ie – check out the 'lighting calculator'.

37

MAKE YOUR LUNCH

TOPIC/SUBJECT	Lifestyle
EXPECTED SAVINGS OR EARNINGS	€450
TIME REQUIRED	40 hours
LEVEL OF DIFFICULTY	● ● ○ ○ ○

Unless you keep a spending diary, it's virtually impossible to know what you are shelling out for, the exception being people who only pay electronically for anything and then go on to examine their accounts on a basis too regular to be considered healthy.

Something that quickly eats into your pocket is what you eat. If you do a weekly shop and then find yourself throwing out food while at the same time buying lunch most days, there is a dynamic there worth changing. The solution is to make your own food.

WHERE THE PROBLEM LIES

Convenience is … very convenient! If you want to get an idea of just how much we love our convenience foods, look no further than the companies that feed into our love of all things full of fat, salt and empty calories.

Chicken baguettes are tasty, there's no denying that; but for the same price you could eat more abundantly and more healthily, as well as more cheaply. It just takes a little preparation.

If you think you don't spend much on little items here and there, do yourself a favour and download an app for tracking your spending. There are many to choose from and we've listed a few at the end of this chapter.

Taking some time to track all your spending is a great idea. It's something worth doing for a week every year just to remind yourself of how much cash you can bleed out just being a normal person.

HOW TO FIX IT

Karl solved this one because he had to: he's a coeliac and can't eat certain foods, which restricts his choice of places he can eat. Part of how he got around that was to put a barbecue into the backyard at his workplace.

Now he can eat lean cuts of meat, roast vegetables and good fresh food, which, in his opinion at least, is better than what you get at the deli counter. That's before you factor in the savings. Even a small steak will only cost about €3 from the supermarket; add in some rice or potatoes and salad and you can eat like a king for under a fiver.

If you can't do this, there are other ways to achieve a similar outcome. At the end of the chapter we have some links to sites that do recipes for low-cost good food. The main 'fix' in this case is to take a little bit of time to plan ahead and ensure you actually make the food.

Anybody who owns a slow cooker should already know that if you make up a good batch of stew or curry it's painless to top up the pot a little so that you have some left over for the next day (or freeze it if you don't like eating the same thing two days in a row).

There so much food waste in Ireland – as a nation we throw away millions of euros of food every year. This is a mistake. Why not avoid doing that and instead have more money which you can then save or spend on something special or be able to afford something you're doing without?

THE SAVINGS EXPLAINED

You'll still have to pay for the food – there's still no such thing as a free lunch – but you can get a great meal cheaper. If you hate the idea of eating at work because you like to get outside, combine eating your own lunch with going somewhere. Walk somewhere and eat there; if the weather's bad, eat indoors then go out with an umbrella – if you were going to eat out you'd have to do that anyway.

Looking at prices generally, for a decent sandwich you'll spend €3.50 or more (at least in Dublin city centre, where we checked); then you might add a yoghurt or crisps, a bar or a piece of fruit – you probably won't just get a sandwich and nothing else.

That turns your daily lunch spend into €5 or more, and it wouldn't be uncommon to spend twice that amount if you go somewhere to sit down for lunch. So if you blend the two together you'd come up with a weekly spend of about €30.

Now consider that you can eat just as well for about €3 to €4 a day, even if you have virtually the same food. The difference of course is the labour cost (you made it instead of somebody else) and you are not paying for the premises of whatever person or company is renting the building to sell food from.

Your expenditure is now more like €15 to €20 a week. We'll take the higher figure and assume that you save at least €10 (in fact it will probably be more), and that you manage to do this 45 weeks of the year – taking away times when you don't bring in your own lunch or when you are not at work.

That's €450 in the bank that takes little more than a change of habit to obtain.

 TIME *It takes time to prepare and be prepared, so we figure 40 hours a year is realistic. This is almost like an extra week's worth of work in order to eat better and for less. That said, it's a worthwhile endeavour and one that puts you in control of an important part of your health, namely your diet.*

 DIFFICULTY *This plan isn't difficult, but it can be a hassle to stick to. As with anything that requires preparation, the continued dedication can grind you down over time. If you do your best to get to the point where it's just another habit of yours then it will be far easier.*

OK 1K 2K 3K 4K 5K 6K 7K 8K 9K 10K 11K 12K

THINGS TO WATCH OUT FOR *Pre-planning is hard work at the start and gets easier over time as you learn what does and doesn't work. So find a few sites with recipes you might like, think about your shopping list and then introduce the changes.*

USEFUL WEBSITES *For lots of good homemade lunch choices:*
www.eatingwell.com/free_downloads/healthy_lunch_recipes_for_work_cookbook
www.wisebread.com/25-quick-cheap-lunch-ideas
www.thesimpledollar.com/20-favorite-dirt-cheap-meals
Budgeting apps:
http://fudget.dconnell.co.uk
www.mint.com
www.goodbudget.com
www.youneedabudget.com

38
CONVERT YOUR CAR

TOPIC/SUBJECT	Transport
EXPECTED SAVINGS OR EARNINGS	Zero in year one, but €1,000 a year after that
TIME REQUIRED	2 days
LEVEL OF DIFFICULTY	● ○ ○ ○ ○

In Chapter 31 we looked at how you can make your car more fuel efficient and also how spending more on fuel is a common mistake. This chapter is about fundamentally changing the type of fuel you use in order to save thousands.

When we talk about 'gas' (Americans aside) most of us think about home heating, barbecues or patio heaters, but here's an interesting thing – you can run a car on it too, and if you do your fuel prices are cut almost in half; it's the same fuel used to heat homes, but when used in a car it's called autogas.

Here's how it works. You add a second tank to the car, so now it's a 'dual-fuel' vehicle. While this is described as 'converting', it isn't entirely converted – you can run your vehicle on both fuels. The car will still start on petrol but then run on liquefied petroleum gas (LPG). The tank normally goes in the boot where your spare tyre lives. You take the spare out and buy an emergency inflation and repair kit. This shouldn't be too great a concern as many new cars have no spare tyre anyway.

Then a filling point for the gas is installed, typically next to the petrol filling point. There are different connections in different countries: Ireland and Germany use the same; the UK, Spain and other areas have different connections. So if you plan to drive abroad, pick up the one you'll need, which will cost about €15.

Fuel prices may be at historic lows, but that won't stop them going up again, particularly because much of the inflation in energy isn't down to the raw materials, it's the government lashing on the taxes, which you can't avoid.

In economics the demand for fuel is seen as 'inelastic', which in layman's terms means that there will always be a demand for it, no matter what the price is.

WHERE THE PROBLEM LIES

When you buy a car you'll notice that diesels are far cheaper, despite the fact that it's an environmentally dirtier fuel. They do have good engines and run for ever, but the majority of people buying diesel cars don't buy them for their mileage; they like the lower tax and the cheaper fuel.

You may not be able to sort out the tax treatment of vehicles, but if you can buy one for many thousands cheaper because it isn't a diesel, it still takes years of higher tax before you break even. So unless you plan on keeping a car for a very long time it's a false economy not to buy the less expensive petrol one.

Autogas use is incredibly common in mainland Europe: ten million cars in Eastern Europe alone use LPG instead of petrol. It's rising in popularity because it's cheaper; a litre of gas fuel only costs about 65c.

It's so popular that many manufacturers make cars that come out of the factory with an LPG conversion already built in.

A litre of gas is about 15–20% less efficient than a litre of petrol, so on that basis the cost is more like 76c in terms of getting a 'like-for-like' amount of power for your vehicle, but that's still close to half price.

LPG is also VAT-retainable, like diesel (there is never any VAT reclaim on petrol), so this is a way of making a petrol car more tax-efficient if you drive one for a living and are VAT registered.

HOW TO FIX IT
How much does it cost to do the conversion? A good-quality one with the best parts will cost about €1,100, but it can be done much more cheaply if you use cheaper parts, so it depends on what kind of job you want done.

So a tank goes in, the filler point goes in and the gas line is run to the engine. The car starts on petrol every day, but when it reaches a pre-set temperature it switches automatically to gas. If your gas is empty or you run out it will automatically go back to petrol and there is a device that lets you know. No brain is required to use this technology.

How does it work? A vaporiser turns the gas from liquid to vapour – it does to gas what a carburettor does to petrol – then LPG injectors are added to the engine. This is what puts the gas vapour into the engine. The gas tank has a computer that ties in with the car's unit so that everything works together.

It's worth mentioning that some cars don't take gas conversions. Some cars with direct injection can't be converted at present, but in time there will be new kits for these cars. The main thing is to call the person doing the conversion to find out more. A chat with them about the type of car you own or are considering and whether or not it will work will answer all your questions.

Some engines will need additional lubricants to protect their valves; again, your conversion installer will advise you on this.

A kit normally lasts as long as the car does; the tank has a ten-year lifespan, and at Car Gas they give a five-year guarantee on their work. It's worth checking any warranty from the garage you bought the vehicle from – some won't cover certain engine issues if you get a conversion. What that means is that, if something goes wrong with your car and it should be under warranty, if the problem has anything to do with the engine they might try to use the conversion as a 'get-out clause'.

THE SAVINGS EXPLAINED

We'll assume you spend about €50 a week on petrol; that's €2,600 a year. So you get a gas conversion done and you now spend about half as much on fuel, but remember, autogas is a little less efficient, so we have some maths to do. Your €2,600 (assuming fuel costs €1.30) will buy you 2,000 litres of fuel a year. You now buy autogas at 65c a litre, but per litre it only gives you 85% of what petrol gives you. The result is that you end up buying more litres to get the same amount of power, so you'll use 2,350 litres of autogas to match the petrol you used to buy. At a cost of 65c per litre you'll have to buy €1,500 of fuel.

Which means you don't make a saving in year one, but you will in year two. For that reason we are going to use that figure – not every good decision is instantly rewarding. The savings in year one are set off against the cost of the job.

 TIME *Getting the work done takes about a day and a half. This gives the installer time to double-check everything. Some companies, such as Car Gas, give their customers a courtesy car to use while the job's being done.*

 DIFFICULTY *This is a fairly simple one. The most difficult part of it is paying for the conversion because you have to do that up front and then absorb the savings over time. You'll also need to find an autogas location within striking distance of where you are – if there isn't one it may not make sense to convert your car.*

 SOME THINGS TO WATCH OUT FOR *As we've mentioned, if you have a car with a standing warranty you might want to talk to the garage. Also, you can't convert your car if you acquired it through a hire purchase or PCP (personal contract plan) deal. You'll also want to make sure that the installer has worked on a vehicle like yours and knows whether it needs additional lubricants or other features that may be required to make it work. More important, get a comprehensive quote for the entire job, factoring all this in.* **USEFUL WEBSITES** *www.cargas.ie*

 Lots of garages that supply autogas are listed at www.myLPG.eu; others are listed at www.flogas.ie.

39

EAT LESS MEAT

TOPIC/SUBJECT	Lifestyle
EXPECTED SAVINGS OR EARNINGS	€200 or more
TIME REQUIRED	Negligible
LEVEL OF DIFFICULTY	● ● ○ ○ ○

There is a health crisis coming down the track and it has a lot to do with our lifestyles. Eating too many calories, in particular sugar and low-nutrition fast food, is a prime issue, but there are other contributory factors.

You've probably heard the expression 'your health is your wealth'. Well, you can work it in reverse – your wealth is contingent on your health. When people talk about their income or their wealth they are really talking about the greatest asset anyone will ever own.

That is your time. While a house may be a large store of wealth once you pay off the mortgage, the biggest asset you'll ever own is all your earning capability over your life. This is what gives you the capacity to make money, invest, save and become wealthy. It's a slow burn, too; the majority of people who achieve decent wealth do it slowly.

That's why an obesity crisis and low-nutrition diets are such an issue; they take away from your earning ability through shortened life, poorer health and other issues. We've seen in Chapter 35 that losing weight is a money-saving tip.

Another common problem is waste, Britain's Food Standards Agency (FSA) did estimates which boil down to an average family throwing out about €1,000 of food a year. Irish families waste €700 worth of food every year, acoording to the Environmental Protection Agency.

WHERE THE PROBLEM LIES

Meat is one of the most consistently expensive food items, even in an era of industrial farming. It's pricey because of the high standards of Irish meat production, with safeguards such as end-to-end (farm to fork) traceability being the norm.

Then there is the fact that growing plants, then giving the plants to animals to eat so we can harvest the livestock, uses a lot more fuel, water, chemicals, medicines and fertiliser per calorie of food produced than just eating the plants ourselves. The waste products can also be a source of pollution and a large part of why Ireland has such a high level of CO_2 emissions is down to farming, in particular dry stock farming.

This isn't an anti-farming rant, or a 'meat-is-murder' view; the simple fact is that the amount of meat the average person eats per year (USA statistic) has almost doubled since 1961. It is likely a similar figure in Ireland where affordability and national tastes are strongly centred on the likes of beef, lamb and pork.

Leaps and bounds are being made in laboratory-made meat and some day we might find that we no longer have to kill animals to enjoy meat.

The reality right now is that we waste a lot of food, and if meat is the dearest thing on the menu, which also shows up in our bins, then eating less of it translates into less food waste of meat and that in turn is a money saver.

Obviously households with dogs may never have to consider throwing out meat or scraps, but for those without a secondary mouth to feed this is a good money-saving tip.

HOW TO FIX IT

Don't forget, the reason we are told to eat our 'five a day' or other such numbers is because we tend not to. When did you see a piece of health advice saying 'don't forget to treat yourself to the chipper every few weeks' or to 'eat meat and remember to drink some alcohol'.

Just eating a little less meat has some big upsides. A National Cancer Institute study of 500,000 people found that those who ate the most red meat daily were 30% more likely to die of any cause during a ten-year period than those who ate the least amount of red meat.

Sausage, luncheon meats and other processed meats also increased the risk – horrible news for Karl, who loves his meat and in particular a nice big grill on a Sunday morning. Those who ate mostly poultry or fish had a lower risk of death.

Incorporating this change into your life has many benefits, only some of which are financial. Obviously, it may help increase health and longevity (the good kind of longevity, where you age 'better' than the rest of your peer group). Then, if you have less meat, some of which might end up in the bin, you have higher odds of both eating it all and not wasting any; this also saves money.

We're not saying you should become a vegan (unless you want to), but If you want to cut back, just a little or a reasonable amount, here are some ideas. First, eat more vegetarian meals per week. This, for Karl, is literally a vision of hell on earth, so if, like him, you can't face the thought of it, try the second choice, which is to reduce the size of your portions of meat. This is also a good way to still enjoy more expensive cuts occasionally.

Try eating offal – it's some of the most nutritionally dense parts of the animal. Some ancient cultures actually turned up their noses at the meat we relish today, instead prizing cuts like liver, heart and kidney. They can take some getting used to, particularly since they are no longer part of many popular diets, but that just means you have to be a little inventive.

Make each person's portion of meat smaller than usual, and add another vegetable or bean side dish. You can easily adopt a way of food preparation that is common in China, where obesity levels were traditionally far lower – simply fill out a dish with more vegetables and nutrient-dense foods.

If you want a reminder of why it's a good idea and the health elements aren't swaying you, think about this; animal agriculture is estimated to produce more greenhouse gases than the whole of the transportation industry combined. Reducing or eliminating your meat intake can have huge implications for climate change.

Another argument is that millions of animals are killed each year for meat, with a huge number of these being raised in factory farms. Switching to a less-meat or no-meat diet is a reasonable contribution towards reducing the cruel treatment of animals. While Irish farms are held to high standards, not all the meat you eat is from Ireland and for that reason you don't know how the animals were treated.

On top of this, meat has become so packaged that few people can relate to the fact that a living creature had to die in order to provide its body for you to eat. Karl thinks that everybody who eats meat should have to personally kill an animal once in their lives to ensure they see the link between the two. This would reduce meat wastage. (Here's hoping he never gets his way!)

THE SAVINGS EXPLAINED

Let's say that you find yourself throwing out a cut of meat, be it processed or raw, that has reached its 'best before date' or you bought it because there was a two-for-one deal, or you cooked just a little too much and yet not enough to make usable leftovers.

If that is the case it's very possible that you have thrown away €2 or more per week. If you didn't spend the money on meat and instead bulked up meals with cheaper, nutrient-dense foods, or ate the odd vegetarian meal, you could save not just this €2 but another €2 per person on a meal that didn't contain meat. You could quickly find yourself saving about €5 per week. Over the course of a year this can add up to €250 or thereabouts.

In order to give a conservative estimate we are going to say that the savings could be greater than €200; for bigger families it will be more. Obviously, if you are already a vegetarian you can munch some tofu in anger that this tip doesn't apply to you, but don't worry – we have other ideas that will work for you, whatever you like to eat.

TIME *Eating less meat is not really a time creator or destroyer, it's merely a shift in how you prepare the meals you are going to consume anyway. The main difference you ought to see is a slightly lower food shopping bill. If you also look for slightly cheaper cuts of meat or alternative cuts (for instance stewing beef as opposed to lean steak for a stew) you'll also save on the meat you do buy.*

DIFFICULTY *It can be tricky to change your diet. So much of what people like depends on what they grew up with or what they find 'normal', just as a visitor who never tried a Guinness or doesn't know how black pudding is made would be confused and possibly disgusted. Getting used to eating more vegetables and alternative proteins can take time and it will definitely take some dedication, but the good news is that you still have to eat, so you can't avoid the necessity either way – it's about moving it just a little bit in a different direction.*

SOME THINGS TO WATCH OUT FOR *It can be hard to transition if you start using all new recipes because invariably this will mean messing things up the odd time, and that can turn into the wrong-minded outcome of 'I don't like eating less meat' when in fact a badly executed recipe will come out badly, no matter what the ingredients are. So give yourself time and start with just one meal a week, then do two, then three and so on.*

USEFUL WEBSITES *http://www.jamieoliver.com/galleries/15-veggie-recipes-to-make-meat-eaters-envious/*
http://cookieandkate.com/2016/24-meatless-recipes-that-carnivores-love/
http://www.lifehack.org/articles/lifestyle/these-30-vegetarian-recipes-are-good-you-might-rethink-meat.html
http://allrecipes.com/recipes/253/everyday-cooking/slow-cooker/
http://www.countryliving.com/food-drinks/g1186/vegetarian-recipes-0309/
http://www.delish.com/cooking/g3849/best-slow-cooker-recipes/

40

INHERITANCE TAX

TOPIC/SUBJECT	Tax breaks
EXPECTED SAVINGS OR EARNINGS	€3,000 a year
TIME REQUIRED	1 day
LEVEL OF DIFFICULTY	● ● ● ● ●

There are only two certainties in life: death and taxes. That is the famous quote from one of the founding fathers of the United States, Benjamin Franklin. And the two certainties are linked when it comes to inheritance tax. The big certainty about inheritance tax is that if you do not have a plan, and you own or receive assets, the risk is that you will end up paying inheritance tax. And we have a rather high inheritance tax rate of 33% in this country. Many people deeply resent this, as they feel it is a punishment for prudence. People who have spent their life using their taxed income to build up and pay for an asset like a home are not be best pleased to see a chunk of the value of that asset ending up in the hands of Revenue when they pass it on to the next generation. The bottom line is that if you fail to prepare, then prepare to pay inheritance tax when it comes to passing on assets at death.

WHERE THE PROBLEM LIES

A wife, husband or civil partner can inherit from their spouse or civil partner without paying inheritance tax. Everyone else has to pay the tax. The official name for inheritance tax is capital acquisitions tax, sometimes referred to as CAT. This tax can be broken down into two types: a) gift tax, which is payable when a person giving the gift is still alive; and b) inheritance tax, which is payable when the person giving the gift has died.

There are tax-free thresholds, but amounts over these mean you are liable to pay CAT at a wallet-busting rate of 33% for anything over these threshold amounts. This is one of the highest rates in the western world. But it should also be noted that the tax-free thresholds are reasonably generous for sons and daughters who inherit. The other tax-free thresholds are low if the giver has no children. Different tax-free thresholds apply depending on the relationship between the person giving the gift (the disponer) and the beneficiary. The tax applies on all property in Ireland. It also applies if the property is not in Ireland, but the person giving the benefit or the person receiving it is resident in Ireland for tax purposes. However, even with the tax-free threshold, an only child inheriting a house worth €400,000 from parents in the tax year 2017 would face a bill of €29,700.

The tax is calculated based on the market value of the inheritance on the date of death. To calculate your inheritance tax liability you take the value of the asset at death. You then subtract the tax-free threshold amount from this. What is left is taxed at a rate of 33%. It is worth noting that you can deduct any liabilities, costs and expenses that are properly payable from the value of the asset. These might include debts that must be paid. For example, there may be funeral expenses, the costs of administering the estate, or debts owed by the deceased. For a gift, they could include legal costs or stamp duty, according to information on the tax from the Revenue Commissioners and the Citizens Information Board.

The tax can become even more expensive if you are late paying it. This is known as a surcharge and applies to the late paying and filing of CAT. The surcharge is calculated as a percentage of the total tax payable for the year the return is late. It goes up, depending on the length of the delay. The only good news on this is that there is a cap on the level of the surcharge. For someone who is no more than two months late, the surcharge is 5% of the tax due, up to a maximum of €12,695. If you are more than two months late, the surcharge is 10% of the amount due, up to a maximum of €63,485.

HOW TO FIX IT

There are three ways to either avoid the tax or lessen its impact. Your options are to ensure you use the tax-free thresholds, avail of exemptions, or benefit from a relief. Evading the tax is not something we would advise. Getting good professional tax advice is something that is certainly worthwhile, especially if there is a likelihood the benefits being passed on will exceed the tax-free thresholds in value.

When it comes to tax-free thresholds, there are three different groups. Different tax-free amounts apply to each group.

- Group A: the person receiving the gift is a child of the person giving it. This includes a stepchild or adopted child. It can also include a foster child in certain circumstances.
- Group B: the person getting the gift is a brother or sister, nephew or niece of the giver, a grandparent, grandchild or great-grandchild.
- Group C applies to any relationship other than those in Groups A and B.

The annual gift exemption means you can receive gifts of cash worth up to €3,000 a year tax-free. And this does not count when calculating the inheritance tax-free threshold, according to solicitor Susan Murphy of Make My Will, a low-cost service for making your will where you provide your instructions via email through a secure service, or you can be contacted by phone at a time that suits you. The annual gift exemption does not apply to inheritances, because the giver is still alive.

Business or agricultural relief may apply to gifts and inheritances of business or agricultural property provided certain conditions are met. It operates by reducing the market value of business or agricultural property by 90%. This means the inheritance tax is calculated on an amount which will be significantly less than the market value.

THE SAVINGS EXPLAINED

Take a home with a market value of €450,000 which is passed on to a son and a daughter. As they have a tax-free threshold of €310,000 each, neither of them will be liable for the tax. This is because they are each inheriting a €225,000 share of the house.

If there is only a daughter who is inheriting a house of the same value, she faces a tax bill. The bill will be the threshold less the value of the house. That means you subtract €310,000 from €450,000. This leaves €140,000. That is taxed at 33%. The bill comes to €46,200.

Now suppose you received a previous threshold from your parents. You were generously given a gift of €20,000 to help you put a deposit together for a house. This will reduce the threshold when the home is inherited.

TIME *This is an area you need to devote time to. Allow at least a day for seeking out information and consulting with a legal or financial adviser if you are passing on assets or receiving them.*

DIFFICULTY *Tax matters tend to confuse people. We recommend you take time on this one, and you would be wise to seek out professional help.*

SOME THINGS TO WATCH OUT FOR *Making a will is advisable. If you die without one, the law on intestacy will decide what happens to your property. Having a will in place will mean proper arrangements are made for your dependants, and they may be able to avoid a hefty tax bill. It will also ensure your assets are distributed in the way you wish after you die, subject to certain rights of spouses/civil partners and children.*

There are fixed dates for paying and filing a CAT return. All gifts and inheritances with a valuation date in the year ending on 31 August must be paid and filed by 31 October. What this means is that if the valuation date is between January and August in any year, you must complete the tax return and pay the tax on or before 31 October that year. If the valuation date is between September and December, you must complete the tax return and pay the tax on or before 31 October 31 the following year, according to Revenue.

USEFUL WEBSITES *The Revenue website (www.revenue.ie) has compre-hensive information, but is difficult to follow. Also worth checking are www.citizensinformation.ie, and www.makemywill.ie.*

41

BUY A
WATER FILTER

TOPIC/SUBJECT	Lifestyle
EXPECTED SAVINGS OR EARNINGS	€20
TIME REQUIRED	A few minutes
LEVEL OF DIFFICULTY	● ○ ○ ○ ○

Everybody knows the benefits of staying hydrated. It's an important aspect of general health and sports performance, and good old oxidane (that's the scientifically accepted name for water) is what helps to carry a lot of waste products out of your body.

Some time ago the trend emerged of bottling water and selling it at a hefty price. When it first began a lot of people thought it was just a fad, but sales in bottled water have been on an upward trend for years now, and many people buy it for home consumption and spend reasonable amounts of money on it.

WHERE THE PROBLEM LIES
Habits, whether good or bad, are habits nonetheless, and if you are in the habit of buying bottled water, you may be spending more on it than you think. So ask yourself a simple question: could you, in a blind test of all types of water, tell which is which?

Often you can tell tap water from spring water or filtered water, particularly if you have a good sense of smell, as you can pick up on the chlorination scent from some waters. But only a connoisseur can tell filtered water from spring water. So why shell out so much?

HOW TO FIX IT
Buying water is a bad idea for a few reasons. Apart from not being good value, it's also of varying quality and some bottled water has very high sodium levels, fluoride (for the people who don't like fluoridation) and chemicals like bisphenol A (BPA), which can leach from plastic containers into the water. Obviously this doesn't happen with glass bottles, but those waters tend to be the most expensive – which supports the idea of ditching bottled water even more.

Don't blow money on bottled water. Instead, just get a glass, metal or BPA-free bottle, and a filter, and you'll save money and have all the water you need.

THE SAVINGS EXPLAINED
If you buy a jug on sale you'll pick one up for about €15. Like printers, where companies make money on the toner cartridges, the filter companies tend to make a lot of their income from the filters, so first find the cheapest filter supplier you can, then get the jug that works with those filters rather than going for the cheapest jug first.

We'll say that you buy two bottles of water a week in a shop (or even a multi-buy in the supermarket). If you were to spend about €2.50 a week on them, that's expenditure of €120 a year (assuming you do buy water 48 weeks of the year).

If you can source a jug for about €15 and use about €30 worth of filters in a year, the savings is €75.

As with many of our estimates, we account for somebody who is a 'heavy user', but you might almost never buy water or you buy very little, so your savings would not be as big as we have figured.

For that reason we are going to stick with a net save of about €20. If, based on your knowledge of your own consumption, you reckon it's less, then you'll know yourself that it isn't a worthwhile tip. But if you do drink bottled water regularly it should deliver you €20 or more in savings.

 TIME *This tip can be sorted out in a few minutes; once you get your filter you just have to get into the habit of using the jug.*

 DIFFICULTY *It's not at all difficult – just remember to fill your water bottle!*

 SOME THINGS TO WATCH OUT FOR *The main thing to be aware of is the refills – that's where people who have followed this tip say they have been stung. Find cheap filters and buy the jug to go with it; don't do it in reverse where you buy a cheap jug, as you may find out later it has the most expensive filters that you'll have to replace regularly.*

 USEFUL WEBSITES *Go online and find a Brita jug on sale. (Brita is a well-known manufacturer of water filter jugs.)*

Check www.argos.ie and other sites like eBay, Amazon and any other online marketplace, many of which will offer jugs and replacement filters.

42

SELL AND DECLUTTER

TOPIC/SUBJECT	Lifestyle
EXPECTED SAVINGS OR EARNINGS	€100 or more
TIME REQUIRED	6 hours
LEVEL OF DIFFICULTY	● ● ● ○ ○

Having some clutter in your life is a totally normal thing. The rise of clothing collections exist for this very reason. What isn't the best idea is to hold on to lots of clutter and never do anything about it.

The reason you ought to do something about it isn't just about cleaning out the clutter from your life; there is a financial reason too. Chances are you are sitting on several hundred euros worth of something that you're not using yourself and you're missing out on selling it to somebody who actually does want it.

Try to remember that when you bought something you spent your money on it. While you can't get all your money back (most things depreciate rather than appreciate), you can perhaps claw back some of it, and that's a really great idea.

A famous story did the rounds on the internet a few years back (it's a true story, too – the link is at the end of the chapter) about a guy who started off with a single red paper clip and through barter, smart exchange and guile eventually turned that single virtually worthless item into a two-storey house.

He had two important skills: the ability to sell; and a good eye for striking deals. Being able to sell is one of the most valuable skills in life and Karl thinks it should be a school subject (perhaps the tamer 'negotiating skills' might work).

To sell you need to be able to understand value – that means being able to appraise something – then you have to know your market and then do the work of getting in front of potential customers.

The internet has taken care of a lot of this for you, and advertising sites are an ideal place to do this.

WHERE THE PROBLEM LIES

The main issue for most people is that getting your act together to do this takes a bit of effort and time and letting the status quo persist is highly tempting.

The other issue is not realising just how expensive the things you own are to replace. Ask anybody who has made an insurance claim and they will tell you that you simply never account for everything. This, along with a view of things that were paid for in the past being a 'sunk cost' (the view that because the money was spent it is no longer recoverable), make for an easy oversight for most people.

But you wouldn't leave money sitting on a table for a stranger to take, so why let it sit on the table in your own home and not make use of it?

There is an important idea to get hold of when it comes to personal finance because it encourages action. The idea is that when through inaction you don't better your own position it's the same as giving money away to a stranger – better yet, imagine giving it to somebody you don't like.

If you can grasp that thought you'll be well positioned to understand any financial issue that takes a little effort and be spurred into action because while charity is important, giving money away to strangers for no reason (the equivalent to what we are saying doing nothing is) is not that important.

HOW TO FIX IT

The first part of this solution is to look around you and make a short list of all the things you have that you don't use any more. Obviously we aren't talking about heirlooms or things with sentimental value.

Next you have to learn to appraise them – this means putting a value on them. Avoid the 'endowment effect', a tendency to view what you own as being worth more than somebody else would value it.

How do you avoid that? You use a comparative method. To do this you do two things: first, look up the retail value of the item when it is brand new; second, look at the price of the item sold second hand by looking at websites where it might be listed.

Now there are two broad approaches: sell at or below minimum price to get a fast sale; or go for a price around the same as similar items, and wait. If your item is in particularly good or bad repair you may need to adjust your price. The offers you do or don't get ought to give you a good idea of whether you are in the right ballpark.

After coming up with a price, advertise the item (some well-known websites are listed at the end of the chapter); then it's a case of selling the item, accepting or rejecting offers and completing the transaction.

Before you start, go on YouTube and find a video on how best to take pictures of things for sale – it does make a difference. If what you are selling has particular elements that you'd look out for in real life, make it easy for a buyer to see the same thing. For instance, if you're selling a guitar, you'd want to take pictures of the neck and scratch guard. If a potential buyer turns up and then sees that they're badly worn, you've wasted everyone's time, but if they know (from the picture) the state of the guitar in advance they will still be interested.

After that you just repeat the process. You can get an app for your smartphone and manage it all from there. Selling things you don't use any more can be a passive form of income, and you're also decluttering your house (and your life!).

Things people often have to sell are CDs, video games, instruments, sports equipment, machines, parts of things that aren't usable because some other part isn't working (for instance, bike wheels from a bike with a broken frame).

THE SAVINGS EXPLAINED

The savings in this case are going to be more in the form of 'earnings' because what you are doing is taking latent wealth and transforming it into cash. How much or how quickly really depends on the person, so it isn't easy to give an exact sum or amount. What we have figured is that with some creativity – even if you decided to just sell old clothes by the kilo (there are places that buy them) – you ought to be able to do a big clear-out and turn your old items into €100 or more.

 TIME *We figure that to get your accounts set up, take the time to organise the things you want to sell, list them for sale, then reply to people will take about six hours, end to end.*

 DIFFICULTY *This can range from very difficult and time-consuming to relatively easy, it really depends on how you approach it, how serious you are and how much time you want to dedicate to it.*

 SOME THINGS TO WATCH OUT FOR *When starting off you'll make some mistakes. Perhaps you'll spend too much time on time-wasters or you might even have to deal with people who are not entirely honest. Use common sense and make your personal security a priority, particularly if you're selling valuable items.*

 USEFUL WEBSITES *Check out sites like www.donedeal.ie, www.adverts.ie or www.gumtree.ie. Also keep an eye out in your area for car boot sales, where you can also sell off unwanted things.*
The red paper clip guy: http://oneredpaperclip.blogspot.ie/
Other useful ideas:
http://lifehacker.com/5981335/the-complete-guide-to-selling-your-unwanted-crap-for-money
http://www.clark.com/where-to-sell-your-old-stuff-for-top-dollar
http://fieldguide.gizmodo.com/how-to-sell-all-the-stuff-you-dont-need-online-1784635255

43

SAVE WITH BANANAS

TOPIC/SUBJECT	Lifestyle
EXPECTED SAVINGS OR EARNINGS	€15
TIME REQUIRED	1 hour
LEVEL OF DIFFICULTY	● ○ ○ ○ ○

A comedian (apologies to whomever it was – we can't recall who said it) once had a skit about Irish people and their fruit bowls. It went something along the lines of 'Some cultures buy fruit and actually eat it, unlike in Ireland where we buy loads of it and then wait until it's rotten and throw it all out.'

We decided that we'd have to have at least one chapter in this book that wasn't too serious, but which also did have some factual financial advice in it too.

Did you ever find yourself throwing out bananas? If so you are probably very normal.

WHERE THE PROBLEM LIES

There are issues with bananas in how they are collectively bought and the prices received by the farmers who grow them. It's a social cause well worth reading up on, but that aside, in terms of food wastage they are a fruit that is regularly thrown out.

One report by the business intelligence firm Retail Active showed that single men are the biggest food wasters (around €25 per month) and that the banana is the most thrown-out food.

So if we can prevent or reduce the amount of the nation's most popular fruit that's thrown away, surely it has to be a good thing?

HOW TO FIX IT

For a start, you can use black bananas in things like banana bread. Any chef or baker will tell you that the blacker the banana the better the banana bread. If you want to start eating less sugar you can cook with bananas as an alternative to sugar (look up flourless banana brownies for inspiration) and many recipes specifically call for bananas that have gone beyond the point when people would normally eat them.

The main tip, though, is one you probably haven't heard. It sounds wacky but it actually works. Wrap the stem of the banana in clingfilm – or, if you want to recycle, use the light plastic bag you often get at the supermarket, tear it up and wrap it around the banana stems. Doing this really increases their shelf life.

It has something to do with the spread of ethylene gas which the stems release. For the best results, separate the bananas and wrap each stem in clingfilm. The clingfilm will cost about 1c per bunch but will save you throwing out a banana or two per week.

THE SAVINGS EXPLAINED

We are estimating that you spend in the region of 20c per banana. If you save one or two a week (by not throwing them out) you will either end up buying fewer or having them for longer and not throwing them out. Either way, it's a fair assumption to say you might save one and a half bananas a week, which is 30c a week and approximately €15 a year.

| 0K | 1K | 2K | 3K | 4K | 5K | 6K | 7K | 8K | 9K | 10K | 11K | 12K |

Because bananas are compostable we aren't going to assume you also end up putting out the bins less, although if you live in an apartment or don't have a composter you may well make some negligible savings on waste too by not using the bin, or brown bin if you have one.

No matter how you do things you will reduce your waste and carbon footprint by wasting less food, so think about the full suite of issues because the annual savings available here are a little too low for this to be something you'd be sure to do every time.

 TIME *Over the course of a year it shouldn't take more than an hour to implement this tip. It's easy, and you can do it as you put the fruit away when you get home.*

 DIFFICULTY *A brain donor could do this one in their sleep, so go bananas (pun intended) ...*

 SOME THINGS TO WATCH OUT FOR *If after this you still find yourself throwing out fruit, you may be buying too much or doing the thing we all do – swearing you'll eat fruit as a snack but instead hammering the pack of chocolate digestives you bought at the same time. Solution: don't buy the junk food and actually eat the fruit.*

 USEFUL WEBSITES *You can find articles online explaining how the clingfilm solution works if you care to find out more.*

44

LEARN TO HAGGLE

TOPIC/SUBJECT	Lifestyle
EXPECTED SAVINGS OR EARNINGS	€150
TIME REQUIRED	1 hour
LEVEL OF DIFFICULTY	● ○ ○ ○ ○ or ● ● ● ● ● depending on the person!

Most of us don't dwell on the idea that modern market economies are so amazing because we have readily accessible 'prices' and some level of uniformity in them. For most of human history this was not the case; prices had to be agreed and there was no consistency across the country. For instance, milk costs about the same amount in every county in Ireland, but that wasn't the case in the past.

The tip in this chapter is haggling: it's an enduring art and one that should be in any person's arsenal in order to get good value because sniffing around for a deal will only get you so far; after that the art of haggling comes in. Karl thinks Irish people are naturally gifted modern-day 'horse traders' and they know their way around striking deals better than many other nationalities.

Whether this is true or not doesn't matter. What matters is whether it applies to you, and if it doesn't, how you can change things so that you have the requisite skills should you find yourself in need of them.

WHERE THE PROBLEM LIES

Price tags (in law they are an 'invitation to treat') have taken care of a lot of the work of figuring out prices for consumers. Before there were price tags you would have had to go to different suppliers, find out their prices, then figure out which deal was the best. The internet has done away with a lot of that, to the extent that it is ridding people of any incentive to haggle because margins on sales are already thin and then there are no humans to haggle with.

The other big barrier is a social one that is becoming more common-place – people are afraid or too embarrassed to ask for a better deal when buying something. Some people say that asking for a further discount than any advertised price is mortifying. Our view is that it's more morti-fying to be willing to pay more for something than you need to.

There is a right and wrong way to go about haggling, and we'll explain some of the pointers next.

HOW TO FIX IT

First, be mannerly. The idea that to haggle you have to be offensive is some kind of misguided carry over from the Middle Ages when people arguing about prices might lead to accusations and the drawing of swords. Obviously we don't want to see things go any further than polite discussion, so be fair and courteous – don't stray from that starting point. Also don't be afraid to have some fun with it. A lot of things in life are only fun if you can find the fun in them, so see it as a bit of a challenge for yourself.

Now the list:

1 Be nice. If you've ever worked serving another person you'll already know that it's so much easier to give people a better deal when they are nice; in fact, our initial tip of being mannerly plays into this to the extent that you can almost be sure that if you aren't mannerly you'll be terrible at haggling.

2 Show enough interest in whatever you are considering to let the other person know that you can be convinced to purchase, but only if the deal is a good one. In this case 'good' means better than whatever price is currently being offered.

3 Use language people in sales can relate to. 'Knock a few quid off that, will ya?' is more like a command and doesn't give them the clearest signal. A really clear signal would be, 'I'm in a position to buy that today if you can do me a better deal.' When you've made that proposition, shut your mouth. Salespeople (and people in general) aren't comfortable with silence, so whatever they say next should give you a good indication of where you stand.

4 A common (and very effective) rebuttal is, 'I can't – there's no margin on that', to which you reply, 'That's a pity. I was [note the past tense] ready to buy, but that price is above my budget.' Thank them for their time but don't walk away; start browsing something else. Having worked in sales, Karl knows that it's just too hard for salespeople, who naturally like closing deals, to resist trying to reopen negotiations.

5 Standing your ground is vital. If you can't do this, don't get into haggling. Another tactic is to let the person selling the goods give an indication of where the price floor is. If you make the first offer and they instantly say 'yes', you'll never know how much you left on the table.

6 The art of good negotiation isn't to vanquish the other side as if they are an opponent; you want to ensure that everybody wins and gets something but that you benefit to the maximum degree.

7 Another way to haggle is to accept a price but to ask for extras, so if you were buying a computer you could ask for some software or extra RAM or other feature. On cars you could ask for longer warranty or better extras for the same price.

8 Know your enemy. With cars, a good time to buy is when people are not buying, and the same goes for houses – there is often some seasonality in the market. With other goods, such as white goods, staff have monthly targets and a big purchase can be attractive at the start of the month to help a person get a good start or at the end of the month when they might want to get their numbers up in order to hit a target.

Retailers of every type have really upped their game. There are offers for almost anything that are regular and generally well priced, but we don't want our readers to be like everybody else – we want you to do even better. So haggle. Promise yourself you'll haggle on something within the next month.

THE SAVINGS EXPLAINED

It's hard to determine how much you can save by haggling because it really depends on what you buy, but there are virtually no limits to what you can haggle on. People haggle on houses, cars, insurance – you can haggle on almost anything other than bus fares (in Ireland, that is; in other countries people do haggle with the bus driver) and groceries, which may be possible, it's just that neither of us has ever seen it done.

 TIME *Unless you are in fairly protracted negotiations on a really big-ticket item, haggling need not take up much of your time.*

 DIFFICULTY *This depends on the person. Some of us are born hagglers, some are willing to learn it; others, despite knowing the savings they could make, simply cannot bring themselves to haggle. Try to remember that haggling doesn't make you a cheapskate; being a cheapskate makes you a cheapskate. Haggling over something you care about should be more like a badge of honour!*

 SOME THINGS TO WATCH OUT FOR *Unless you are willing to walk away, you are in a weakened position, so when you go to haggle, be in a position where you are ready and willing to buy something but you don't have to, otherwise any decent salesperson will spot that a mile off and you are done for. For example, if a mechanic knows your car has broken down and you are trying to negotiate the price on a fix, the chances are you won't do a particularly good deal because they know you are a compelled purchaser.*
   Good luck with it!

USEFUL WEBSITES *Just search for 'haggling tips' and remember, if you go into a retail shop with live people in it then you can haggle. No matter what they tell you about prices or margins, you can haggle, no two ways about it.*
https://www.fluentin3months.com/negotiation-tactics/
http://www.artofmanliness.com/2011/05/11/how-to-haggle-like-your-old-man/

45

AVOID VAT

TOPIC/SUBJECT	Tax breaks
EXPECTED SAVINGS OR EARNINGS	€50
TIME REQUIRED	30 minutes
LEVEL OF DIFFICULTY	● ○ ○ ○ ○

Long-standing structural issues mean the cost of living in this country is sky high. The small nature of our economy, poor levels of competition, lax regulation, high taxation and the power of vested interests combine to ensure that householders often get very poor value for money. We have one of the highest standard value added tax (VAT) rates in the world. At 23%, our standard VAT rate is a fifth higher than the international average. A high VAT rate pushes up the cost of shopping. The higher, or standard rate, as it is known, applies to a huge range of goods and services, including baby powder, telephone bills, detergents, non-oral medicines, car parts and IT equipment.

WHERE THE PROBLEM LIES

Our high VAT rate is one of the reasons consumer prices in Ireland are among the highest in the EU. The level of prices here in 2016 was the second highest in the EU, according to figures from Eurostat. Prices were 25% above the EU average in that year. Ireland had the fifth smallest increase in inflation in the EU between 2011 and 2015, but prices remain high by EU standards, the CSO said in a 2017 report called 'Measuring Ireland's Progress 2015'. However, consumers can take some small consolation from the fact that even though prices here are 25% above the EU average, this represents an improvement on 2008. Back then price levels in Ireland were 30% above the EU average and were the second highest in the EU.

Ireland has the eighth highest VAT rate in the world. Our standard rate of 23% is a fifth higher than the international average. The rate is set by legislators, not the Revenue Commissioners. The standard rate in Ireland is not far behind Hungary, which at 27% charges the highest VAT in the world, according to a report by the Organisation for Economic Cooperation and Development (OECD). A high VAT rate makes it more expensive to run a home. But it is also important to point out that reduced rates of VAT introduced by many countries often benefit the rich more than the poor.

HOW TO FIX IT

The key thing to remember about VAT is that it is designed to hit you as soon as you spend in a shop. It is an effective sales tax, from the exchequer point of view. But the good news is that you can make savings around the anomalies of VAT. It is worth remembering that there are a number of different rates of VAT. The main ones are the standard rate at 23%, a 13.5% rate, a 9% rate, and a 0% rate. Having a good with a 0% means there is no tax imposed for consumers, but the supplier has to record goods sold at this rate in a VAT return.

Some things are exempt from VAT, so restricting your purchases to VAT-free goods could make your life a lot cheaper. Mostly it is impossible to avoid paying VAT. Evading the tax is illegal, and not something we advocate. But there are some ways to ensure you do not pay the tax – by buying goods and services that are VAT-exempt or ones that are zero rated for VAT. These include buying children's sizes in clothes and shoes, buying physical books as opposed to downloads, and ordering low-value items online, according to good research done by personal finance journalist Louise McBride and published in the *Sunday Independent*.

THE SAVINGS EXPLAINED

There is a 9% VAT rate on paper books and other printed material, but if you download a book to read on your Kindle, iPad or smartphone you will be hit with a VAT bill of 23%. There is zero rate of VAT on school books and children's picture, drawing and colouring books. However, do factor in that you might still pay less for a Kindle book than a paperback – even if the VAT is higher for the Kindle.

You don't pay any VAT on clothes that are labelled, marked or marketed as being for children under 11 years of age. After that, you're hit for 23% VAT. So if your child has a smaller build than average, take advantage of that – don't be tempted to buy clothes labelled for an 11-year-old for your ten-year-old if they will still fit into clothes for their age. Likewise, if your 11-year-old is petite enough to fit into clothes for a ten-year-old, stick to the younger size.

It is a quirk of the system that ballet, gymnastics and Irish dance lessons are exempt from VAT, if they are part of a programme that meets standards set out by the Department of Education and Skills. You pay 23% VAT on adult swimming lessons, but lessons for a pre-school or school-going child are VAT-exempt.

When you order a meal in a hotel, consider ordering fruit juice instead of bottled water. You pay 23% VAT on any alcohol, soft drinks or bottled waters you have with a meal. The VAT rate on fruit juice is just 9%.

It's worth noting that VAT at the zero rate applies to flour, eggs, sugar, butter and buttermilk. So if you make scones at home, tax is not one ingredient you need to use. But if you buy scones in your local café you will have 9% VAT added to the cost. In fact, you pay 13.5% VAT on most of the cakes and desserts you pick up in your local supermarket or bakery.

When it comes to biscuits the tax authorities take different-sized bites depending on the variety of biscuit or snack. Chocolate-covered biscuits are taxed at 23%. Plain biscuits have VAT levied at 13.5%, but VAT at the zero rate applies to baby biscuits. A bag of microwave popcorn doesn't attract VAT because, according to the Revenue Commissioners, 'it is not suitable for human consumption without further preparation'. You'll pay 23% VAT, however, on a bag of ready-to-eat popcorn.

Cold food is a good option if you want to avoid the tax, as the zero rate applies. You do not pay any VAT on cold food, such as a sandwich, or frozen food, such as a frozen pizza. However, once that food is heated up, you'll pay 9% VAT. So if you want to minimise the tax you pay, instead of picking up a pizza in your local takeaway, buy it frozen in your local supermarket and heat it up at home.

 TIME *It should take no more than a few minutes to memorise a few items that are either exempt from VAT, subject to VAT at the zero rate, or have the lower rate applied to them.*

 DIFFICULTY *It is not easy to know what VAT rate applies to different goods and services, or if there is an exemption. But noting some of the low or VAT-exempt rates can save you money.*

 SOME THINGS TO WATCH OUT FOR *You can buy goods (except tobacco products, alcohol or perfume) from outside the EU up to the value of €22 without incurring any VAT charges. If it is over this amount, and comes from a country outside the EU, you generally have to pay VAT at a rate of 23%. VAT of 23% and varying levels of excise duty apply to alcohol and tobacco products delivered here, even if excise duty was paid in the EU country of origin.*

 USEFUL WEBSITES *The Revenue Commissioners has extensive infor-mation on VAT rates on its website, at www.revenue.ie/en/tax/vat/.*

46

GET OUT
OF DEBT

TOPIC/SUBJECT	Banking
EXPECTED SAVINGS OR EARNINGS	€000s
TIME REQUIRED	8 hours
LEVEL OF DIFFICULTY	● ● ● ○ ○

The financial crash that began in 2008 has left people in this country with a legacy of debt, and many people are struggling with unsustainably high levels of borrowing. Recent figures show that adults here are the third most indebted in the EU. The average amount of consumer debt per person in Ireland is now €31,216, according to Central Bank of Ireland figures. We may be paying it down at a fast rate, but we are still a heavily indebted nation. The borrowings come in different shapes and sizes: credit card balances, personal loans, mortgages and debts associated with investments that went wrong. Many of us are living on borrowed time, but sooner or later we have to deal with borrowings if the situation has gone out of control.

WHERE THE PROBLEM LIES

The household debt burden in Ireland remains huge. Many can cope with their debts, especially if they have retained their jobs, have a low-cost tracker mortgage, and acted early to restructure the payments. But the debt legacy of the banking and economic collapse remains an intolerable burden for many thousands of households. Often, these people were not reckless; banks pushed too much debt at them and then dramatically changed economic circumstances rendered their situation untenable. The improving economy is doing little to improve the situation. If your debts are out of control, falling unemployment and more jobs will help, but it may not make this problem go away. The government-funded Money Advice and Budgeting Service (MABS) reports that the number of people seeking advice has fallen from the sky-high levels during the worst of the crisis four years ago. However, the complexity of household debt problems are, if anything, deepening. Not only is unsustainable debt a massive threat to your financial wellbeing, it is also an enormous mental health challenge. Indeed, the situation has overwhelmed many, with tragic results.

The Citizens Information Board provides a useful set of criteria to assess whether your borrowings have become a problem. You know your debts are out of control when you are:

- missing payments and getting letters from creditors;
- only paying the lender that is putting the most pressure on you;
- borrowing money to pay bills or to eat into arrears;
- overpromising creditors to meet payments when they contact you;
- breaking those promises repeatedly;
- getting legal letters from creditors.

The good news is that there are lots of options for the heavily indebted, and there's a lot of free advice on offer.

0K 1K 2K 3K 4K 5K 6K 7K 8K 9K 10K 11K 12K

HOW TO FIX IT

The first thing to do is to assess the situation. Work out exactly how much you owe and to which institutions. Also establish what you are paying each creditor at the moment. Try to get a handle on what interest rates you are paying on your different debts.

Once you have done this, you need to attempt to work out the value of your assets. This is to see if your assets are more or less valuable than your liabilities. If you have a mortgage, attempt to find out from the local estate agent your home's approximate value. This will tell you if you are in negative equity – a situation when you owe more than your property is worth. Remember that property values have increased lately – so you may be pleasantly surprised at your home's worth. You also need to include other items such as pensions, investments and any savings, according to advice from David Hall of the Irish Mortgage Holders Organisation. Now calculate the monthly household income, including the likes of child benefit and any extra payments coming into the home.

Time-consuming and head-wrecking though it may be, it is important to do the sums to get a firm fix on just how bad your debt situation is at the moment.

Your next move is to seek expert help. Initial meetings are often provided at no cost. Seek out a personal insolvency practitioner (PIP). By law they have to be regulated by the Insolvency Service of Ireland. Other options include a debt management professional, but only if they are regulated by the Central Bank, or a debt charity. An excellent option is MABS. Vouchers for free financial and legal advice and help from experts are available through MABS.

A consultation with any of these will be very useful for discussing your options. These people know their way around the system and the rules of engagement. And remember, it is never too late to get assistance.

The Insolvency Service of Ireland administers a number of formal debt deals. These arrangements have to be approved by the courts, giving them the force of law. They include:

Debt Relief Notices (DRNs)

If you have a **low income, few assets and debts of less than €35,000** that you can't repay, a DRN could be the right solution for you. Your adviser (also known as an approved intermediary) will deal with your creditors on your behalf, putting an end to any demands for unpaid debt – no more phone calls, letters or visits. A DRN will last for up to three years. After that time the debts named in your DRN will be completely written off.

Debt Settlement Arrangements (DSAs)

If you have a large amount of **unsecured debt** that you are unable to pay, such as credit cards, loans and overdrafts, a DSA could be an option. A DSA is a formal agreement with all your creditors that will write off some of your debt. Your professional adviser (also known as a personal insolvency practitioner) will deal with your creditors on your behalf, putting an end to any demands for unpaid debt – no more phone calls, letters or visits. Under the DSA you agree to repay a percentage of your overall debt that you can afford in monthly payments over a given period of time.

Personal Insolvency Arrangements (PIAs)

If you have **secured debt and unsecured debt**, such as a mortgage, that you cannot repay, a PIA may be a way to get on top of the situation. A PIA is a formal agreement with all your creditors that will write off some of your unsecured debt and restructure any remaining secured debt. Your qualified professional adviser (also known as a PIP) will negotiate with your creditors on your behalf, putting an end to any demands for unpaid debt, according to the Insolvency Service.

Under the PIA you agree to repay a percentage of your overall debts that you can afford in monthly payments over a given period of time. While you are making these repayments you are entitled to a reasonable standard of living. You will not be told how you should spend your allocated reasonable living expenses, so you are still in complete control of your spending.

Bankruptcy

Bankruptcy is a formal High Court process for people in debt over €20,000. Before you consider applying for bankruptcy you must first have explored the alternative solutions to bankruptcy outlined in the previous few paragraphs. If these alternative solutions are not suitable, bankruptcy could be the solution. When you are declared bankrupt, your property and possessions are transferred to a person called the official assignee, who arranges for those items to be sold. The money generated from the sale is distributed to the people you owe money to – your creditors.

THE SAVINGS EXPLAINED

Restructuring your repayments, cutting an informal deal with your lenders or seeking a court-approved insolvency arrangement will save you a large amount of money, and ease your worries.

TIME *If your debts are large, there is no getting away from the fact that dealing with the situation is going to be time-consuming and complex. You would be wise not to set a time limit on it and be aware that it may take you weeks, even months, to get back on an even keel financially.*

DIFFICULTY *Tackling huge debts is a challenge of mountainous proportions. Like the advice about how to eat an elephant, take it one step at a time.*

SOME THINGS TO WATCH OUT FOR *Once you get on top of your debt situation it is important to be disciplined. This involves meeting the terms of new agreements you have in place and avoiding taking on new borrowings. You would be wise to cut up any credit or store cards so that you can't use them. Get rid of your overdraft facility. But also remember that most banks operate a 'shadow' overdraft service, according to the 'money doctor' John Lowe. This allows you to overdraw by an amount of around €500 before the bank contacts you. You will eventually have to formalise this arrangement, and so will end up with an overdraft facility in place by stealth. Try not to buy unnecessary items. Is that bargain really something you need to purchase? Pay with cash when you can – we are slower to spend the folding stuff than flash a plastic card at a retailer.*

You would be well advised to avoid some of the financial adviser sharks out there.

USEFUL WEBSITES *There is a lot of information online, but be careful of firms trying to make money out of your misery. Good independent advice is to be found on the MABS website, www.mabs.ie. The Insolvency Service of Ireland has a user-friendly website outlining the options for insolvency deals and the process around bankruptcy at www.backontrack.ie.*

47
WELFARE FOR FAMILIES

TOPIC	Tax breaks
EXPECTED SAVINGS OR EARNINGS	€000s
TIME REQUIRED	2 hours
LEVEL OF DIFFICULTY	● ● ○ ○ ○

Welfare payments for middle-income families? What's this nonsense? Sure, welfare is only for those out of work, or the poor, you might be thinking. You would be forgiven for thinking we have lost the run of ourselves. But bear with us for a bit. The truth of the matter is that welfare payments for families in this country are so generous that when child benefit and tax provisions are taken into account, a family with two children, on the average wage, is a net beneficiary of the system. And don't take our word for it. That is the view of the international think tank, the Organisation for Economic Cooperation and Development (OECD). The Paris-based organisation points out that child benefit is generous in Ireland. For two children you get €280 in child benefit in 2017. 'Taking into account child-related benefits and tax provisions, the employee net tax burden for an average married worker with two children in Ireland was reduced to 0.2pc in 2014, which is the lowest in the OECD, and compares with a reduction to 14.8pc for the OECD average,' said the OECD in a recent tax trends report. In other words, a family with two children gets back roughly what it pays into the system. But don't think of it as welfare. Think of it as making a claim to the Department of Social Protection for the pay related social insurance (PRSI) everyone in work has to pay.

WHERE THE PROBLEM LIES

The OECD argument is that an average married worker with two children in Ireland had take-home pay, after tax and family benefits, of 99.8% of their gross wage compared to the OECD average of 85.2%. However, it is worth pointing out the dangers of like-for-like comparisons with other countries. It's also worth noting that couples in Ireland face high childcare costs that are subsidised in other countries. The OECD data includes PRSI contributions, but does not take account of other taxes faced by families, including property tax and other charges.

Given all that, it is worth spelling out that welfare for families comes not just in the guise of child benefit. Families on low incomes benefit from the Family Income Supplement, and all families, where there is a stay-at-home parent, are entitled to the home carer's tax credit.

HOW TO FIX IT

Make sure you get every payment your family is entitled to receive. Between child benefit, a medical card, the home carer's tax credit and family income supplement, the direct payments from the State to families are generous in this country.

THE SAVINGS EXPLAINED

Child benefit (previously known as children's allowance) is payable to the parents or guardians of children under 16 years of age, or under 18 years of age if the child is in full-time education, Youthreach training or has a disability. Once the child reaches 18 years of age it is no longer paid.

Let's assume most families that are entitled to child benefit are getting the payment. But a large number of families are entitled to a key tax credit aimed at families, but are not claiming it, namely the **home carer's tax credit**.

The home carer tax credit is not just for those caring for other people's children, the elderly or disabled people. Many people don't realise that it can be claimed where any housewife or househusband works in the home, caring for their own children. Strictly speaking, it is not a welfare payment, but we have included it as it is a significant benefit for families. The tax credit is worth €1,100 in 2017. A tax credit is basically an amount of tax that you do not have to pay. The home-carer's tax credit is available to any jointly assessed couple with one or more child, where the spouse has income of less than €7,200. However, if you work part-time and earn more than this you may still qualify for some of the tax credit.

Maternity benefit is another social welfare payment which women are entitled to for paying PRSI. It is paid by the Department of Social Protection for 26 weeks, two of which are before the baby's birth. The rate in 2017 is €235 a week. A generous employer can pay you your full salary. In that case you are likely to have to refund the employer the benefit. Income tax is charged on maternity benefit payments, but not the universal social charge (USC) or PRSI. However, if maternity benefit is your sole income you will not have to pay tax on it. You need to apply at www.welfare.ie for the benefit between two and 16 weeks before the delivery date.

Paternity benefit is a payment for employed and self-employed people on paternity leave from work, and who are covered by PRSI social insurance. It is paid for just two weeks and is available for any child born or adopted on or after 1 September 2016. You can start paternity leave at any time within the first six months following the birth or adoption placement. You should apply for the payment four weeks before you intend to go on paternity leave (12 weeks if you are self-employed). If you are already on certain social welfare payments, you may get half-rate paternity benefit. The weekly rate from March 2017 is €235.

One-parent family payment is a means-tested benefit payable to those caring alone for children under seven, and earning less than €425 a week, including any maintenance payments. The rate is €193 per week plus €29.80 for the child.

Family income supplement (FIS) is a weekly tax-free payment available to married or unmarried employees with children. It gives extra financial support to people on low pay. You must have at least one child who normally lives with you or is financially supported by you. Your child must be under 18 years of age or between 18 and 22 years of age and in full-time education.

To qualify for FIS, your net average weekly family income must be below a certain amount for your family size. The FIS you receive is 60% of the difference between your net family income and the income limit which applies to your family. If you are getting FIS you may also be entitled to the Smokeless Fuel Allowance and the Back-to-School Clothing and Footwear Allowance.

No matter how little you may qualify for, you will still get a minimum of €20 each week.

TIME *It will take just a few hours to claim child benefit from the Department of Social Protection, the same for the home-carer's tax credit from the Revenue Commissioners, and the same again when it comes to making an application for family income supplement from the Department of Social Protection.*

DIFFICULTY *Claiming these benefits, and the tax credit, is not difficult. Contact your local Citizens Information Board office if you are unsure what to do, or need forms to fill out.*

SOME THINGS TO WATCH OUT FOR *Once you qualify for family income supplement, it will be paid for 52 weeks while you are employed. At the end of the 52 weeks you can re-apply for it if you continue to be eligible. If your wages go up or your spouse starts work, your family income supplement will not be reduced until the end of the 52 weeks.*

USEFUL WEBSITES *A good place to start is www.citizensinformation.ie, which is far easier to follow than the websites of Revenue (www.revenue. ie) or the Department of Social Protection (www.welfare.ie).*

48

TRAVEL INSURANCE

TOPIC/SUBJECT	Holidays
EXPECTED SAVINGS OR EARNINGS	€50
TIME REQUIRED	2 hours
LEVEL OF DIFFICULTY	● ● ● ○ ○

You need to pack a lot of stuff when you go on a trip abroad, but no sensible traveller should leave home without travel insurance. It covers you if you become ill or have an accident while you are on holidays or travelling. Those travelling within the European Economic Area (EEA) (basically the European Union plus Iceland, Liechtenstein and Norway) should have a European Health Insurance Card (EIHA). This allows you to access public healthcare services. But you will need travel insurance to supplement the EHIA card and to cover trip cancellations, theft of personal goods or trip delays. Travel insurance is relatively inexpensive, and has avoided the supercharged premium rises that have hit health and motor cover. As many as half of Irish people who travel abroad do so without putting travel insurance in place. This is a mistake, as the cost of medical treatment abroad can be prohibitive, even if you have an EHIA card. Sometimes non-nationals are charged more for medical treatment as it is assumed that they have travel insurance and they will have no alternative but to pay up. It's worth noting that the most common reason for a claim is trip cancellation. With an outlay of around €100 for year-round cover for a family, cost should not be an excuse for not taking out travel insurance.

WHERE THE PROBLEM LIES

Many people take a risk and go on holiday without travel insurance. Others believe they have adequate cover, when they have bought a cheap policy that has so many exclusions that it is virtually worthless.

Another problem is that people with health insurance assume that they do not need travel cover. Many health insurance policies do include 'emergency cover while abroad' to the value of between €55,000 and €100,000. But the danger is that if your medical costs exceed these limits, you will be personally liable for the difference. Treatment for a minor cardiac problem in the USA could cost you €40,000.

According to insurance expert Dermot Goode of Total Health Cover, you may need to provide a deposit of up to €2,500 on your credit card before you are treated in a medical facility abroad. And daily treatment costs can be up to €1,000 a day, he says. He also warns that some health insurance policies will not cover you for treatment abroad.

Older people need to be aware that ageism is rife when it comes to travel insurance. Often those over the age of 65 will be charged more than those who are younger. This means it will pay for older people to research the market well.

Exclusions are plentiful. Take the cover offered by some airlines. They typically do not cover cabin bags, which they say are the responsibility of the customer. So if your suitcase has a laptop in it and it gets damaged in the hold, hard luck. The airlines say this exclusion is clearly stated in its terms and conditions, which each customer agrees to at the time of booking. This means that when considering which policy to take out it is worth downloading a copy of the terms and conditions and doing a search for the words 'exclusions', 'not covered' and 'excluded' before signing up.

Policies sold by tour operators and airlines tend to be more expensive and have more exclusions than others. Consumers should be aware that natural disasters will not be covered by travel insurance. Insurers see these as 'acts of God' and exclude them from most forms of insurance.

Watch out for large excesses. This is the amount you have to pay before your cover kicks in.

HOW TO FIX IT
The best bet is usually a multi-trip policy for the whole family. This covers you and your family for a year, but there are also now two-year multi-trip policies. If you have health insurance, you will get a discount on the cost of the cover.

Dermot Goode recommends you contact your travel insurer and your health insurer prior to travelling to double-check the following:
- Are pre-existing conditions excluded on the policy?
- Is there an excess that you need to be aware of before you make a claim?
- Are all the places on your itinerary covered by the policy?
- Dental cover is often limited on these policies and may only apply in emergencies. Make sure you check your cover with the insurer.
- Most policies are designed to cover hospital admissions only. If you are treated in an A&E facility but not actually admitted to the hospital, you could run up a sizeable bill which you will be expected to pay. Always have a credit card and check this element of your cover with your insurer.

THE SAVINGS EXPLAINED
Travel insurance is not expensive, unlike other forms of insurance. This does not mean you should abandon getting value for money, but it does mean that you should ensure that you get cover that will provide you with a decent level of cover should something go wrong.

OK 1K 2K 3K 4K 5K 6K 7K 8K 9K 10K 11K 12K

TIME *Spending just two or three hours ensuring that you buy a good travel insurance policy will pay dividends. Cheap, off-the-shelf policies are often not worth it as they are usually riddled with exclusions and excesses.*

 DIFFICULTY *Taking out holiday insurance is not difficult. What will take a bit of effort and some mental endeavour is working out what is and is not covered by your policy.*

 SOME THINGS TO WATCH OUT FOR *Make sure you know what restrictions and exclusions apply before signing up to a policy. You may be surprised by what is not covered on the cover you are offered. People planning to undertake risky sports, such as sky diving or scuba diving, on holiday need to ensure that they will be covered if anything goes wrong. Many policies exclude activities like these. You may need a specialist insurance policy for high-risk activities like bungee jumping.*

If you have any pre-existing conditions, you may find that many travel insurance policies will not cover you, according to the Consumer Protection and Competition Commission. Alternatively, an insurer may cover you for certain illnesses but charge you a higher premium.

Something to watch for is how long you are going to be away. Some single-trip policies will only cover you for 30 to 60 days, so if you are going to be on a long trip you will need long-stay cover.

A key thing to do is to take out the policy on the date the holiday is booked, and not on the day your break begins. This is because you will have no cover if you have to cancel the holiday and your cover does not kick in until the holiday is due to start.

 USEFUL WEBSITES *The website www.consumerhelp.ie has a basic outline of what travel insurance entails. The representative body for the industry, Insurance Ireland, has a decent outline of the cover at www.insuranceireland.eu – search for Travel.*

49

AVOID HOLIDAYS FROM HELL

TOPIC/SUBJECT	Holidays
EXPECTED SAVINGS OR EARNINGS	€1,000
TIME REQUIRED	6 hours
LEVEL OF DIFFICULTY	● ● ● ○ ○

We look forward to our holidays. They offer a chance to get away from home and change our routine. The thought of sipping a nice local wine at a beach restaurant over a relaxing meal is enough to put you in a good mood in the days leading up to the break. But if you do not plan your trip well, sunburn could be the least of your worries, and instead the trip could end up burning a hole in your pocket. You need to plan ahead to ensure your break does not turn into a financial nightmare.

WHERE THE PROBLEM LIES

We drop our guard when we are on holiday. We shift down a gear or two, which means we are vulnerable to being overcharged, and because we're not used to coping in hot weather we are liable to make costly mistakes. Being away from familiar surroundings also means we are susceptible to scam merchants. The dangers can come from anywhere: from hidden charges and extras you were not told about when booking your holiday, to sneaky fees for car hire you were not told about in advance, to the nightmare of being a victim of theft.

HOW TO FIX IT

You can reduce the risk of having a holiday from hell by taking a few precautions. Then the worst you will have to deal with is a little too much sun. Here are some key tips.

Travel insurance

As we saw in Chapter 48, travel insurance is a necessity for those going abroad. A basic policy should cover you for emergency medical expenses, lost and stolen money or personal property, recompense you for cancelling or cutting your trip short due to an insured reason, and cover you for missing a flight due to an insured reason. But holidaymakers should be aware that the travel insurance they take out may not offer all that they expect. Some policies have exclusions and get-out clauses. Some policies cover hospital admissions only, and will not refund the cost of using an accident-and-emergency facility.

Don't assume you have comprehensive cover for something going wrong by spending just €50 on a policy. You would be well advised to check before taking out the policy if you will be excluded from treatment for a pre-existing condition. It is also worth being aware of how high the excess is – this is the amount you have to pay yourself when you make a claim. Note, too, that it is cheaper to take out travel cover if you already have a health insurance policy. Experts generally recommend you need at least €2.4m worth of medical cover in place.

When it comes to theft, make sure the conditions can be complied with, as insurers will avoid a pay-out if they can. Avoid taking an insurance policy from the holiday company you are booking with – you will usually get a better deal if you shop around online. If you don't get travel insurance, at least get the European Health Insurance Card (EHIC), which is free from the HSE – the details are at www.hse.ie. It will cover you for hospital treatment abroad, though not for an air ambulance home.

Currency
When you travel outside the eurozone, even if it is only to Britain, getting a good deal when you procure foreign money is important. The cost can vary significantly depending on where you acquire your foreign currency, especially for large amounts of money. The two key factors to take into account are the exchange rate you are offered when you buy currency, and the commission on the transaction. It may be worth checking the wholesale rate, known as the spot rate, before you buy your currency. Check out websites like www.xe.com. This information is likely to help you get a better deal. Currency exchanges in airports are often the worst place to get your foreign cash. Institutions can often be competitive on one currency, but not on another. Places you should check out to see if they offer value include An Post, your bank, and Fexco Click and Collect.

Car hire
Hiring a car has been described as a money trap, and for good reason. Car hire companies are notorious for trying to impose extra charges and attempting to get you to sign up for extra insurance cover when you pick up the vehicle – this is the very time your resistance is at its lowest as you want to get the car and go to your destination. So be aware of hidden charges and extras which could turn a 'cheap' daily rate into an expensive road trip. When you rent a car, the standard insurance included normally features a large excess, which can be as much as €2,000. Rental firms have a reputation for imposing large charges for even small dents. The car hire company will try to persuade you to take out the car hire company's own excess insurance. This can be expensive, with costs of €300 for two weeks not unusual. You would be wise to buy a stand-alone car hire excess insurance policy before you travel. The

likes of www.carhireexcess.ie offer this cover from €2.99 a day. AXA also offers this product. When you collect the car, it is very important to check for pre-existing scratches and dents, and take pictures with your phone as proof. When dropping off the car, try to get a rental firm employee to sign off on its condition, or at least take more pictures yourself.

And you should be clear about the policy on whether you return the car with the fuel tank full or empty. If you do not meet the correct condition, you can lose out financially.

ATM use outside the eurozone

You would be wise to limit your use of ATMs outside the eurozone. This is because the costs are high. There are typically minimum charges that apply. And there are often charges imposed by the local ATM provider, especially in the United States. Add in the fact that you typically get a poor exchange rate, and you have the makings of a bad deal. This means that it is best to keep visits to ATMs in countries that do not use the euro currency to a minimum. If you must use your debit or credit card to withdraw cash from a machine, take out a large amount. This is because you are charged per transaction. But there is an obvious security risk if you are carrying around something like $1,000 in cash. Anther option is to buy a currency card. One of these is the An Post FX card. This operates like a chip-and-pin debit card. You pre-load it with the currency you need and the amount. You can fund the card in sterling, US dollars, Australian dollars or Canadian dollars. There is no charge for the card and when it is used in a foreign ATM machine the charges tend to be lower than those on your own bank card. However, local ATM charges are likely to still apply. You can top up the card online from anywhere in the world.

Fly midweek

Opting to fly on a Tuesday or Wednesday means you will pay less, as demand is lower for flights. Deciding not to depart at the weekend could save you a few thousand euros. It's also worth considering avoiding travelling in July and August if you can. Of course, this only applies if you do not have school-going children. Families locked into the school holiday schedule often end up paying €1,000 more than those who opt to go on holiday in May or September.

Know your rights on flights

Thanks to the EU, consumers in Europe have some of the strongest protections in the world. Cancelled and delayed flights are a pain, but thanks to EU regulations there is a responsibility placed on airlines to look after customers affected by delays. Usually, this involves getting you on another flight. Alternatively, the airline can offer you a refund or pay for hotel costs, meals and some telephone calls while you wait. You may also be entitled to financial compensation for lengthy delays. If the airline does not offer you redress you deem sufficient you can complain to the Commission for Aviation Regulation. See www.aviationreg.ie.

THE SAVINGS EXPLAINED

Ensuring you have a good travel insurance policy in place, getting a deal on your foreign currency, avoiding the pitfalls of hiring a car, and minimising your use of ATMs abroad are among the best ways to avoid being overcharged. It's also worth considering flying midweek, and you would be wise to be aware of your rights under EU regulations.

 TIME *It is worth taking time to plan a holiday well and ensure you have the likes of your finances and car hire in order ahead of the trip. It will only take a few hours to do this.*

 DIFFICULTY *None of what we have outlined here is difficult. The big challenge will be to allocate the time to doing it.*

 SOME THINGS TO WATCH OUT FOR *It is worth remembering that in some countries you may be asked for identification when use your debit or credit card. And be warned that your bank may, for security reasons, reduce the amount of cash you can withdraw each day from an ATM outside the EU. It would be wise to check this limit with your bank before you travel.*

Sometimes when you use a debit or credit card outside the eurozone you are given the option of paying in euros or the local currency. This is known as dynamic currency conversion. Say you buy something in England and the person processing your card at the check-out asks you if you want to be billed in euros. In general, it is cheaper to pay in the local currency (sterling in this case), according to the Competition and Consumer Protection Commission.

0K	1K	2K	3K	4K	5K	6K	7K	8K	9K	10K	11K	12K	

USEFUL WEBSITES *The aviation regulator, the Commission for Aviation Regulation, has good user-friendly information at www.aviationreg. ie. For help resolving cross-border disputes in the EU, try the European Consumer Centre's website at www.eccireland.ie. The Competition and Consumer Protection Commission has information on car hire, using bank cards abroad and travel insurance at www.consumerhelp.ie.*

50

THE WHOLE
PICTURE

At the beginning of this book we said that it was worth €25,000, and we accept that some readers will never reach that total sum because we started with the belief that nobody could make every financial mistake we describe.

There are others who will do better because they will be able to use more of the tips, and most importantly, some of the big ones. Imagine a person who uses help-to-buy at the same time as room rental and they also quit smoking? Just using those three can put them way over the estimated €25,000 mark.

That said, we all (Charlie and Karl included) make certain choices, or avoid certain choices, that go on to cost us in some way. These choices can be directly about how you earn or spend your money; they can be small decisions you make regularly such as what you do with your spare time or the foods you eat.

All these choices create different consequences in your finances, your earnings and your health. What we wanted to do was to highlight some of these things in a way that would make it easy for you to figure out your way through them without having to spend your life doing what your authors did, namely reading and researching these things most of your waking hours for years on end.

We accept that there are also things that people know they are not doing right and which they will continue to do. Karl did, does and will continue to buy takeaway coffee because that's his vice (although he did finally get a percolator at work recently).

If you are doing something that negatively affects your finances and you know you are unlikely to change the way you are doing it, at least after reading this book you ought to be aware of it and you can consider making an adjustment somewhere else in your spending to make up for it.

So let's say that you decide you don't want to stop buying takeaway coffee. Perhaps instead you can focus more on quitting smoking or think harder about taking on another income-generating activity by turning your hobby into something that pays you.

Money is an emotive topic, and it always has been. For most of us the feeling of wanting 'more' of it isn't really about the love or desire of money in itself, it's more about wanting the things it gives you, which is really a series of choices.

If you don't have any money you often have far fewer choices: fewer choices in what you do, how you do it, where you go. If you had enough money you could decide to never work again or to go and live on a yacht. Of course, you could also decide not to do any of those things, but the point is that it would be your choice.

The majority of people never get to make choices like that; they are instead stuck with a certain set of circumstances and it takes time and effort to change those circumstances and rise up from where they start.

One of the wonderful things about this is that it's precisely what people often tend to do. In Ireland we don't always have the relevant statistics, but in the USA they do track people through their working lives and they have found that almost one in five who start off in the bottom decile of income rise into the top decile at some point in their lives.

This is an important point. You should never accept the financial position of today as if it is some kind of immutable thing that cannot change. It can and it does change.

To think that the rich stay rich and the poor stay poor is like thinking that whatever team won the Premier League last year was made up of the same people who won it 30 years ago. The composition of groups changes, so if you hear that over the last 20 years 15% of people have been living on low incomes, don't forget that it probably isn't all the same people being held back and held down all the time.

In fact, many have moved onwards and upwards and they would laugh if you were to suggest to them that they were poor – they may not be rich, but they aren't in the bottom decile any more either. Equally, there are people at the bottom who are doing just fine. If a person makes no money it doesn't mean their partner doesn't, and the statistics often don't show the 'whole household income' when looking at individual incomes and earnings.

The same thing occurs with the minimum wage. This is why studies that look at raising the minimum wage show how it will both reduce the number of jobs for those earning the minimum wage and will benefit richer households more.

Lots of people, whether the president of the USA or a well-known entrepreneur, go bang and fail at something. The difference between them and many other people is that they get right back on the horse and try again. If you're reading this book because your finances are tight, promise yourself that you will make an effort to get back on your own horse and find a more satisfying future.

It may seem like a philosophical point which has no place in a money book, but the mentality behind wealth matters. There are two broad approaches you can take to money. The first is one that has what Karl would call a 'Catholic overtone' – wealth is a type of prosperity which comes with a certain amount of inbuilt shame. The second is the type he prefers to promote – wealth is usually (but not always) achieved by helping other people and that by serving other people in a fair and honest fashion you will naturally do better financially.

This is worth paying attention to if you ever want to ask for a raise. If you have the former view you will feel bad about it or angry if you are refused; with the latter mindset you start off not by merely asking for a raise, but by knowing that a raise is justified because of your contribution to the bottom line, and if you are rebuffed you know that you can either increase that benefit and ask again or go somewhere else. It does tend to remove the angst from the process.

How you think about money is also important. In many families one person tends to 'take care of financial things', and while this is a good example of what economists call the division of labour, it can also allow inferior choices to persist.

Who could be expected to make informed choices if they don't have any idea of how much they have to make the choices with?

Studies show that across the world, couples of any makeup argue over the same three topics. One of them is money. Money plays a strange role in many of our lives. It can be a tool of control or power and for that reason it must be harnessed wisely.

A good example is a person who has kids who, like all children, can be demanding. If you give in to them every time, what is that teaching them about money? Are you helping a child by letting them have access to spending power beyond what they can reasonably digest at their age? Does it encourage an undying materialism or lack of understanding of value for money?

This is a question that will have a different answer for every person who asks it. People who grew up in families who regularly went without may want to ensure their kids or partner 'have it all' or they may want to 'have it all' themselves.

What people do is up to them, but that doesn't mean we can't make the observation that these choices carry consequences.

Even a single person who has nobody relying on them financially still has to rely on themselves. If they spend all their money on holidays and nice things, how will they be wealthy? How will their wealth grow if they never own a home or save for a pension? How will they prepare for old age?

That means that, rather than waiting to make better decisions only if and when you take on the accoutrements of adult responsibility (bills, raising families, being in relationships, debt and personal financial responsibility), better choices should really be a priority for everybody, irrespective of their situation.

One day we'll probably look back at our education system and wonder how we ever let people get through it without ensuring they were equipped with the tools necessary to make better financial choices as they grow up.

Charlie has been writing in the *Independent* on personal finance for years on these issues for precisely these reasons – his articles and pieces about developments in personal finance help to fill a gap that is left by an education system that doesn't satisfy the need for financial literacy.

Karl does the same thing, but he does it more directly with individuals by advising them personally.

A single book can only do so much to help you. The single biggest ingredient in financial success is the individual in question and, as with many things in life, the person has to want to succeed in order to do so.

This means being willing to make the many and various small sacrifices or changes we've described in this book to ensure that you get the desired outcome. That's the real magic of it all – we can only hope to be conduits, or people who open the gate, so that a person is empowered enough to do something for themselves. Whether they actually do it or go on to do some other version of it is entirely up to them.

AFTERWORD

We hope that you enjoyed this book and found it enlightening, entertaining and interesting. At a minimum we hope you found it to be worthwhile and good value for money.

If you have any good tips that we didn't cover, and frankly we know there are bound to be a lot of them, do get in touch. We hope to update this book as time goes by to reflect changes in the law, in the economy and in how different processes work.

Sincerely,

Charlie Weston and Karl Deeter

NOTES

NOTES

NOTES